Elongated Skulls
Of Peru And Bolivia:
The Path Of Viracocha

Brien Foerster

Cover Photo by Marcia K. Moore

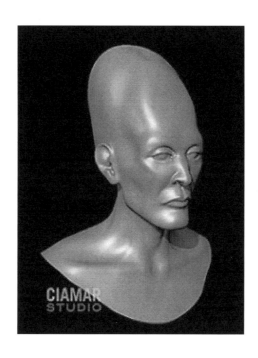

Dedication

This work would in no way be possible without the expertise, wisdom and adventurous spirit of Sr. Juan Navarro Hierro, director of the Paracas History Museum. It was through my relationship with Sr. Juan that the phenomenon of artificial cranium deformation first grabbed my interest, and turned it into a quest. He was born and raised in the Paracas Peru area, and early on avidly pursued the remnants of the fabulous pre-Colombian cultures which had inhabited the area. Sr. Juan is respected by many Peruvian archaeologists for his vast knowledge of the ancient cultures of the Pisco, Paracas and Nazca areas, and in my opinion he is indeed the foremost expert.

I also dedicate this book to Lloyd Pye, known to many for his 12 years studying the strange starchild skull, as well as his questioning the validity of Darwinian evolutionary theory. Though he died at a young age, his contributions to unravelling the mysteries of humanity will never be forgotten.

And last but never least, my thanks to my beloved Irene, whose interest in the mysteries of historical Peru and Bolivia rival my own.

Sr. Juan Navarro and baby Paracas skull

Contents

1: Introduction

2: Peru And Bolivia Focus

3: Viracocha

4: The Path Of Viracochan

5: Below The Path Of Viracocha: Chile

6: Tunupa And Uyuni

7: Potosi

8: Oruro

9: Tiwanaku And Puma Punku

10: Island Of The Sun

11: Sillustani

12: Colca Canyon

13: Andahuaylillas: Huayqui

14: Cusco

15: Ollantaytambo

16: Abancay

17: Ayacucho

18: Inca Wasi And Huaytara

19: Paracas

20: Central Highlands

21: Cajamarca

22: Could Some Elongated Skulls Be Natural?

23: Bibliography

1: Introduction

Permanent alterations of the body such as, dental modifications, scarification, mutilation, tattooing, and piercing, as well as several types and forms of body art and ornamentation have been part of human culture from the beginning of history as a way of differentiating oneself from others. Artificial deformation of the neonatal cranial vault (baby's head) is another example of these types of practices, and is the subject of this book.

Modification of the head's shape, favoured due to the plastic characteristics of the skull in newborns, was carried out by means of a steadfast pressure applied on the head from the first days of life until 2 or 3 years of age, in general. This custom has been found on all continents, except Antarctica as far as we know, and became an especially widespread practice among the cultures of South America, and especially Peru long before the arrival of Spanish conquerors in the 16th century AD.

Artificial cranial deformations (called ACD henceforth) of newborns have been carried out since time immemorial. From the archaic Homo sapiens in Australia (1) to modern times, there was almost no place in the world unfamiliar with this practice. The earliest evidence of ACD comes from remains of the Mousterian people from Shanidar in Iraq and dates from the Middle Paleolithic period (approximately 300,000 to 30,000 years ago.) (2)

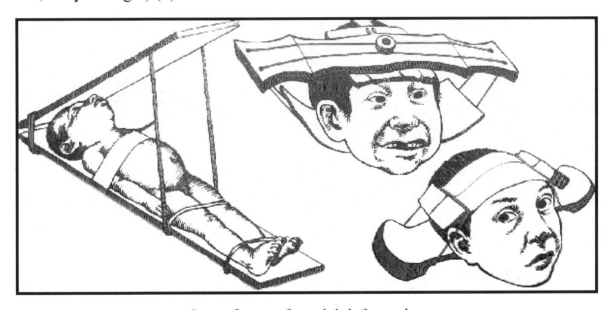

Some forms of cranial deformation

It was already known in Byblos, an ancient Phoenician city, by 4,000 BC and in Georgia by 3,000 BC, and was described by Herodotus (c. 485 to c. 425 BC) in the Caucasus region and by Hippocrates (c. 460 to c. 377 BC) among the people who lived west of the Black Sea. (3) It was a common practice in eastern Asia in what is today Malaysia, as well as Indonesia, Sumatra, Borneo (the Minahassa people), and in the Philippines. In southern Asia, it was common among the Brahuis people in India, in the Punjab region in India and Pakistan, and in Afghanistan, Turkmenistan, and Beluchistan.

Some have suggested that this practice became widespread with the Scythians. This people, pushed out by Chinese emperor Hsuan Wang, had to move from their original settlements in central Asia toward southern Russia into and near the Crimean peninsula in the 8th and 7th century BC. Rich archaeological remains with artificially deformed skulls have been found in excavations just east of this area at the Syr Darya and Amu Darya river deltas.

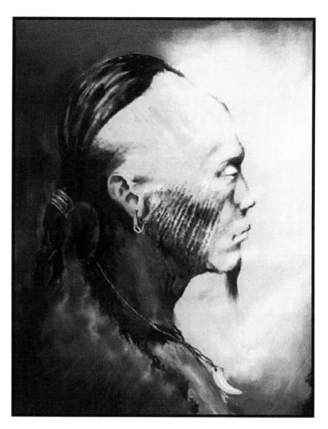

Hun cranial deformation

The Scythians attacked their immediate neighbours, the Cimmerians, and a large-scale nomadic migration toward the west began. The Cimmerians, under Scythian pressure, had to move toward central Europe, staying on the Hungarian plain until about the 4th century BC, when they were invaded, pushed away, and replaced by the Sarmatians until the 4th century AD, when the latter were, in turn, invaded by Hun conquerors. (4)

The Huns, a nomadic tribe of the Asian steppes, were the heirs of the Sumerians and of the Scythians by culture and blood lines. It is interesting to note that the burial rites of both the Scythians and the Huns were quite similar: the same barrows, burial frames of logs and thick timbers, burial blocks, sacrificial horses, etc. In their incursions, the Huns carried their cultural practices, including artificial head molding in newborns, to the whole of central Europe and to the people who had to migrate toward Western Europe. As a consequence, artificially deformed skulls have been found all over the European continent from Romania to Germany (mainly in Hamburg), Austria, Switzerland (near Lausanne), Italy in Genoa and Padua. A deformed skull currently on display at the Padua University Anthropology Museum was found below Piazza Capitaniato in Padua. (5) ACD skulls have also been found in Belgium, France (mainly in the Deux-Sevres and Normandy regions), and in the northern part of the UK.

In Africa, skull deformation was commonplace in Nubia, supposedly in ancient Egypt (Akhenaten is believed by some to have shaped his daughters' heads during the 18th Dynasty, yet no skeletal remains have been found), among the Ashanti tribe in Sudan, other tribes of central Africa, and until not long ago in the Republic of Congo (now Zaire). In Oceania, apart from Australia, it has been detected in Polynesia and Melanesia, especially the islands near Vanuatu. In the case of the latter, oral traditions state emphatically that their dominant blood line, and one could presume such practices as ACD originated in Egypt, though most western academics would beg to differ.

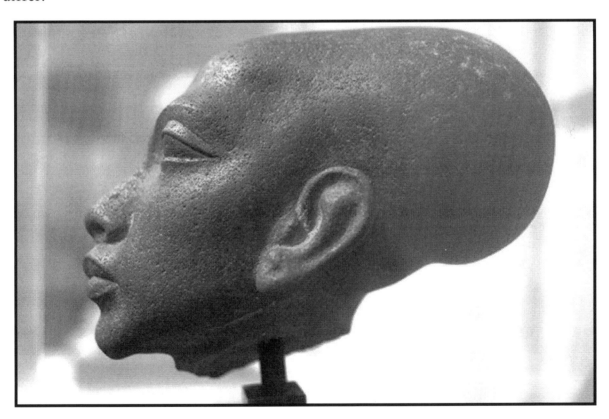

An Amarna period bust from Egypt

The practice of deforming the head in newborns was present in the whole of the Americas, from North America to Patagonia, mainly on the western side of the continents, and especially on the Andean plateau of South America. The expansion of this practice seems to be related to the suggested Asiatic origin of the Native American population, believed to have arrived along the current coasts of Alaska after crossing the Bering Strait, and migrated south from there some 10,000 plus years ago. In North America, it was carried out by the Bella Coola and Kwagiuth of the west coast of Canada, the Flat Head and Pueblo Indians of the United States, in Mexico by the Olmec, Aztec, Huasteca and Maya, and in Central America among the Taino Indians. But cranial molding in neonates was most widely practiced in the Andean region, from Venezuela to Guyana, Colombia, Ecuador, Peru, Bolivia, Chile, and Argentina.

Native American artificial cranial deformation

The current information that exists on this subject is based on reports made by the "chroniclers of the Indias," by travelers, conquerors, and archaeological research, most of the latter having been carried out in the last two centuries. The origin of this practice in the Andean region has been erroneously attributed to the Inca. The ancient Peruvian inhabitants used to mold the cranium in newborns at least 1,000 years before the Inca state was created and started to expand from its capital, Cusco, most likely about 1350. In fact, the artificially deformed skull of a person who lived 6,000–7,000 years BC was found in a cave in Uricocha, in the Peruvian Andes. (6) It was a common practice in the Tiahuanaco (Tiwanaku) state, in the Titicaca Lake region in the Bolivian Altiplano (7) and numerous skulls have been found both at Tiwanaku and nearby Puma Punku.

Later on, as this population expanded, cranial deformation practices moved toward the neighbouring regions, now Peru and the north of Chile. In fact, ACD was recorded among the Paracas people and Nazca people who lived in the south of Peru. We will have a special emphasis on the Paracas in this book, as it has been the center of the author's studies for some years. The Paracas are known, though actual time lines are not well established, to have occupied what is now called the Paracas Peninsula and surrounding area as a distinct culture from about 1000 BC to 100 AD. (8)

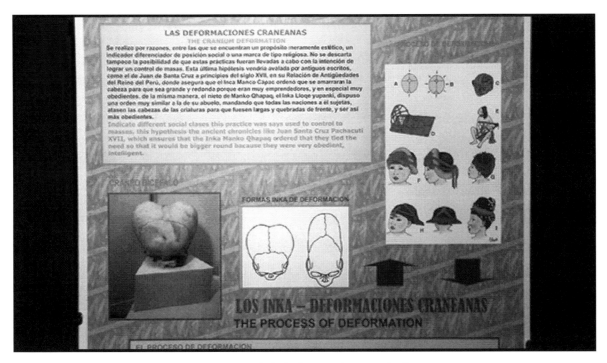

Various cranial deformation techniques

Some indigenous groups in the Arequipa region, also in the south of Peru, used to mold the head in neonates supposedly to resemble the shape of the neighbouring Misti volcano. Similarly, the Indians who lived in the nearby region of Kol'awas used to press the head in newborns with a tight, sharp pointed hat until they progressively adopted the form of the Kol'awata volcano from where the Indians believed they came. In order to differentiate themselves from the Kol'awas, their neighbours the Kawana Kola Indians used to bind the head in newborns with a tight, plaited strand resulting in a flat, wide head very different to that of their neighbours. In a book written between 1590 and 1604, the Inca Garcilaso de la Vega described the boards and bandages technique used by the Palta Indians, who inhabited the north of Peru, to modify the head in newborns. (9)

Intentional deformation of the head in neonates was done in different ways:

1. By compression of the front and back part of the head with boards and pads firmly kept in place by bandages.
2. By tightly wrapping the head with a binding that was progressively adjusted.
3. By restraining the child against a portable cradle board with which the flat position caused occipital compression and an anterior, oblique board that pressed the frontal bone to mold a flattened forehead.

This latter method was introduced by several Indian groups who lived in the northwest of the United States like the Makah and the Plateau Indians in Washington state and Idaho and the "Flat-head" Indians in British Columbia Canada. (10) According to Imbelloni (11) the forms of cranial deformities were the following:

1. Tabular or fronto-occipital: this "flat-head" deformation was an artificial brachicephaly in which the anterior and posterior compression resulted in flattening at the front and back and lateral bulging of the head. Two types of tabular deformations resulted, oblique and erect, according to the angle of board pressure:

    a) Oblique: this head shaping was obtained with two boards compressing in an oblique way the frontal and occipital regions. The compression at the back was centred at the inion and exerted from the lowest part of the occipital bone to the lambdoid suture.

    b) Erect: this type of deformation was obtained in two ways:

        i. By a vertical, frontal piece of wood kept in place by a compressive bandage plus the occipital compression, which resulted in keeping the child flat against the cradle board.

        ii. By two vertical boards exerting pressure on the front and back parts of the child's head. The pressure by the posterior board was centred at the zlambdoid suture, and applied on the upper part of the occipital and back part of the parietal bones.

2. Annular: this was the consequence of tightly wrapping the head with a compressive bandage resulting in a conical cranial vault. Depending on the type of binding, oblique or erect deformations were obtained.

The role and purpose of head shaping varied according to culture and region. In the Andes, head shapes established the person's social identity and separated the different groups within society. (12) In certain regions, ACD was a symbol of nobility or distinguished the ruling classes (13) while in others, it served to mark territory, to emphasize ethnic differences or was performed just for aesthetic, magical or religious reasons.

In large and complex societies, a uniform head shape reflected that the individuals belonged to the same or similar group. In smaller, less complex societies head shape demarcated group differences. (14) The Indians in Oruro, in what is now Bolivia serve as an example of what happened in small societies, where cranial shaping was used for cast differentiation: high class Indians had tabular erect heads, the middle class had tabular oblique heads, and the rest of the people had ring shaped heads.

In the Muisca culture, Colombia, intentional cranial deformation was a sign of hierarchy, performed only in the high classes; it was a sign of social status like clothes, accessories, funeral ceremonies, and tombs. (15) In certain pre-Columbian cultures like the Caribe Indians in Colombia, the Aymara of Bolivia, and the Patagones in Argentina, cranial deformation was performed only on men and it was believed to be an important factor for becoming a member of the so called "warrior class." (16) And yet in Borneo and on the European continent, head shaping was performed only on women with an aesthetic purpose. (17)

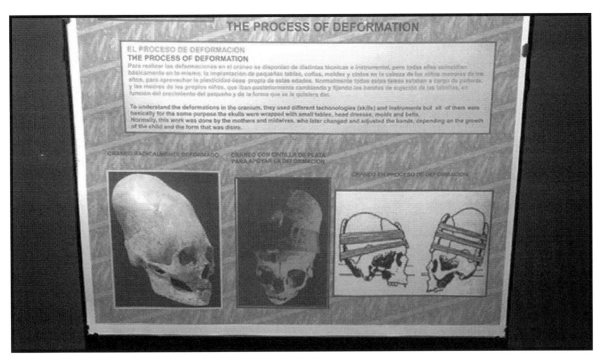

Proposed cranial deformation techniques of the Inca

Among the Calchaqui Indians in the north of Argentina, in the Philippines, and in the Celebes islands, head shaping was performed on both sexes. Some ancient writings linked the purpose of this practice to the intention by certain populations to dominate other people. According to author Santa Cruz Pachacuti, the Inca leaders Manco Capac and L'oke Yupanki ordered the heads of the newborn Aymara Indians to be tightly squeezed to make them foolish, unintelligent, and obedient. (18) The Inca themselves performed ACD on higher classes of their society, and this practice was outlawed by the early colonial Spanish authorities, especially in Cusco at least twice in the 16th century.

However, studies of some indigenous groups who practiced cranial deformation in newborns, such as the British Columbian Indians (19) or the Amazonian natives of South America (20) did not find evidence of any neurological or psychological impairment. It is doubtful that any of the societies who performed ACD would have willfully or even accidentally induced neurological or other damage to their subjects, since in most cases it was the elite classes who had this process done to them.

The first evidence of an artificially deformed skull in Peru was found near Uricocha (Lauricocha), dated to the period between 6000 and 7000 BC, suggesting that the ancient Peruvians introduced the practice on the continent. (21) Lauricocha is located at the headquarters of the Maranon River, in the province of Dos de Mayo, Department of Huanuco more or less in the middle of the country.

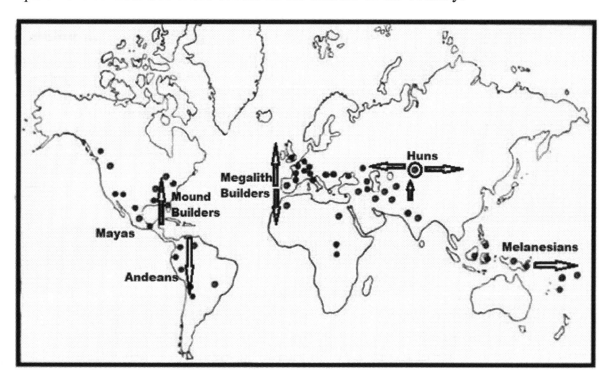

Map of global elongated skull distribution

The elevations there vary from 3900 to 4500 meters. It is believed that this area was favourable for human settlement when the glaciers had thawed at the end of the last ice age. The Lauricocha caves, which are located on an ancient glacial valley in the high regions of Huanuco, apparently housed a large group of hunter gatherers for thousands of years who used the caves as a natural refuge. (22)

Between 1958 and 1960 the Peruvian archaeologist Augusto Cardich discovered in these caves eleven human skeletons; 4 adults and 7 children. The skeletal remains were found incomplete, apparently intentionally mutilated. Lithic (stone) flakes and scrapers, and fossilized bones of camelids (probably llama and alpaca) were also found, along with roots and tubers, shells and bone tools. Rock drawings of animals, depictions of ceremonial dances and hunting were also found on the cave walls. Among the most famous of the burials is the one called "Burial No. 6" with an individual who had artificial cranial deformation of the tabular erect type.

The question naturally arises, if the Lauricocha person is the oldest example of ACD found in South America, how can we be certain that he is actually the oldest that has ever existed? And could this cranial deformation process have independently arisen in the highlands of Peru, and then later influence other cultures? Doubtful. It seems more likely that carbon 14 dating has not been conducted on many Peruvian elongated skulls, and this has led to a major problem in associating them with particular cultures, and relationships between cultures over space and time.

Skeletons in the Lauricocha cave

2: Peru And Bolivia Focus

What this book will address is not only the phenomenon of ACD and its presence in Peru and Bolivia, but the locations where they have been found. There seems to be a relationship between elongated skulls and ancient megalithic sites, in that, where you find very ancient precise stone works, you also, whether in museums, or private collections, also see skulls with ACD. As briefly discussed above, most Peruvian, as well as Bolivian elongated skulls have not been carbon 14 tested, and so any attempts to date them are based on archaeological evidence found at the site of their location. What complicates this matter even further is that the vast majority of conventional academics have in fact made suppositions as to how old the ancient sites and megaliths are. As there has been no way to date cut or shaped stone until very recently, with the invention of cosmogenic testing, the age of a megalithic structure has been based on other cultural artifacts found at that location.

For example, if only pottery from the Inca culture is found at a particular site of interest, then it is assumed that the Inca constructed everything there. Although this sounds like a logical and common sense approach, what if the stone work is in fact so ancient that the archaeologists have not dug deep enough to take the possibility of a greater antiquity into account? Surface exposure dating is a collection of techniques for estimating the length of time that a rock has been exposed at or near Earth's surface. It is used for dating glacial advances and retreats, erosion history, lava flows, meteorite impacts, rock slides and other geological events, and is most useful for rocks which have been exposed for between 10 and 30,000,000 years. (23)

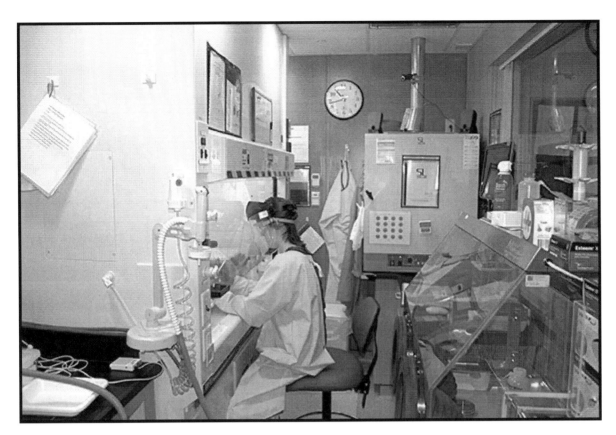
Cosmogenic radionuclide facility

The most common of these dating techniques is *Cosmogenic radionuclide dating*. Earth is constantly bombarded with primary cosmic rays, high energy charged particles, mostly protons and alpha particles. These particles interact with atoms in atmospheric gases, producing a cascade of secondary particles that may in turn interact and reduce their energies in many reactions as they pass through the atmosphere. By the time the cosmic ray cascade reaches the surface of Earth it is primarily composed of neutrons. When one of these particles strikes an atom it can dislodge one or more protons and/or neutrons from that atom, producing a different element or a different isotope of the original element. (24)

The great polygonal wall at Sachsayhuaman

In rock and other materials of similar density, most of the cosmic ray flux is absorbed within the first meter of exposed material in reactions that produce new isotopes called cosmogenic nuclides. Using certain cosmogenic radionuclides, scientists can date how long a particular surface has been exposed, how long a certain piece of material has been buried, or how quickly a location or drainage basin is eroding. The basic principle is that these radionuclides are produced at a known rate, and also decay at a known rate. (25) Accordingly, by measuring the concentration of these cosmogenic nuclides in a rock sample, and accounting for the flux of the cosmic rays and the half-life of the nuclide, it is possible to estimate how long the sample has been exposed to the cosmic rays.

Some archaeological sites which have recently come under great scrutiny as regards their age include Machu Pic'chu, Sachsayhuaman and Ollantaytambo near Cusco Peru, and Tiwanaku and Puma Punku near the southern shore of Lake Titicaca in Bolivia. Machu Pic'chu, Sachsayhuaman and Ollantaytambo are commonly thought to have been completely built by the Inca, and Tiwanaku and Puma Punku by the Tiwanaku civilization. Again, these assumptions are based on the writings of Spanish chroniclers and archaeological methods looking at the artifacts found in relatively shallow excavations. What if deeper digs were performed, along with the use of cosmogenic testing?

The crux of the argument as to why the above sites, or at least portions of them may be older than conventionally believed, and the work of as yet unnamed builders is technical in nature. The megalithic core of Machu Pic'chu, of which the Intihuatana or "hitching post of the sun" is a key aspect, as well as some megalithic elements of Ollantaytambo show levels of technical precision which were most likely beyond the capability of the bronze age Inca. In both places we find mortar free stone masonry in granite so close fitting that in some cases a human hair cannot be fitted in the joints. At Tiwanaku and Puma Punku there are surfaces in hard andesite stone which are as flat as a sheet of glass, most likely not something that the Bronze Age Tiwanaku people could have achieved. And, at all four sites elongated skulls have been unearthed, which have not been radiocarbon dated to my knowledge. So how can we presume their age? Based on surface artifacts?

Massive red sandstone blocks at Puma Punku

What we will do in this book is explore all known locations where elongated skulls have been found, and explore what else has been found at these sites in order to try to decipher who these people were, and when they existed. It will be the work of a future text to examine DNA results of the genetic testing of samples from the elongated skulls of Peru and Bolivia when such data is available. The process is in no way simple nor cheap; to have your own DNA tested from a mouth swab or blood sample is relatively simple now and affordable; for about 100 US you can find out more or less where your ancestors came from, based on the haplotypes which are found. However, the testing of ancient DNA is a far more complicated procedure; since it is biological product, it breaks down rather rapidly soon after death. So, the DNA strands themselves break into smaller and smaller segments over time, and to attempt to recombine their data requires the use of the most modern, sophisticated and expensive DNA diagnostic equipment.

There is a developing pattern in the locations of elongated skulls found in Peru and Bolivia. Most, as has been said previously, are found in any great abundance at or near ancient megalithic sites. And these locations also tend, to some extent to follow a geographic pattern, from central Bolivia towards the border of Peru and Bolivia in a southeast to northwest line. As odd as this may sound, it is a fact.

3: Viracocha

Possible bust of Viracocha

In the ancient traditions of many cultures in Peru and Bolivia, especially the highlands area, east of the Pacific Ocean and among the Andes mountains, there was a teacher, or perhaps a group of them who educated people in sciences, arts, as well as agricultural knowledge. To the Aymara cultures he (or they) was (or were) called Thunupa (or Tunupa) and the Quechua people knew him (or them) as Viracocha (or Wiracocha.)

The Aymara have existed in the Andes in what is now western Bolivia, southern Peru and northern Chile for at least 800 years (or even over 5,000 years, according to some estimations). Their origin is a matter of scientific dispute. (26) The region where Tiwanaku and the modern Aymara are located, the Altiplano, was conquered by Inca ruler Huayna Capac (reign 1483 to 1523), although the exact date of this takeover is unknown. Some linguists have claimed that Aymara is related to its more widely spoken neighbour, Quechua (also called Runa simi, meaning the "voice of the people.") This claim, however, is disputed; although there are indeed similarities such as the nearly identical phonologies, the majority position among linguists today is that these similarities are better explained as features resulting from prolonged interaction between the two languages, and that they are not demonstrably related. (27) In fact, recent linguistic studies indicate that Quechua originated somewhere on the coast of Peru.

Although Aymara people and language are the same thing, Quechua is somewhat different, tending more to describe a closely related number of dialects rather than an ethnic profile.

Relief carving of Viracocha at Tiwanaku

Quechua is a living language to this day, spoken by an estimated 8 to 10 million people in Peru, Bolivia, Ecuador, Colombia, Argentina and Chile. (28) This language had already expanded across wide ranges of the central Andes long even before the Inca, who were just one among many groups who already spoke forms of Quechua across much of Peru. Quechua arrived at Cusco and was influenced by languages like

Aymara. This fact explains that the Cusco variety was not the more widespread. In similar way, a diverse group of dialects appeared while the Inca Empire ruled and imposed Quechua.

The description of both Tunupa and Viracocha is relatively the same in the people of the Aymara and Quechua traditions. The full name and some spelling alternatives of Viracocha are Wiracocha, Apu Qun Tiqsi Wiraqutra, and Con-Tici (also spelled Kon-Tiki) Viracocha. He was one of the most important deities in the Inca pantheon and seen as the creator of all things, or the substance from which all things are created, and intimately associated with the sea. (29)

Viracocha created the universe, sun, moon, and stars, time (by commanding the sun to move over the sky) and civilization itself. He was worshipped as god of the sun and of storms and was represented as wearing the sun for a crown, with thunderbolts in his hands, and tears descending from his eyes as rain. According to a myth recorded by Juan de Betanzos, (30) Viracocha rose from Lake Titicaca during the time of darkness to bring forth light. He made mankind by breathing into stones, but his first creations were brainless giants that displeased him. So he destroyed them with a flood and made new, better ones from smaller stones. (31) Viracocha eventually disappeared across the Pacific Ocean, and never returned but while in the Peru/Bolivia area he wandered the earth disguised as a beggar, teaching his new creations the basics of civilization, as well as working numerous miracles. He wept when he saw the plight of the creatures he had created.

After he left, it was thought that Viracocha would someday re-appear in times of trouble. Pedro Sarmiento de Gamboa noted that Viracocha was described as "a man of medium height, white and dressed in a white robe secured round the waist, and that he carried a staff and a book in his hands." (32) However, de Gamboa was a colonial Spanish writer, and since Viracocha would have lived centuries or even millennia before his time, his description cannot be counted on for accuracy, especially the idea of the "book" as such a concept was mostly likely a corruption of an earlier description by the Catholic thought process.

Carved face of Viracocha/Tunupa at Ollantaytambo

After he created the flood, wiping out the giants which displeased him, Viracocha began his journey, which follows the "path of Viracocha" which was previously discussed. From the Lake Titicaca area he travelled in the direction of the northwest. He arrived at the site of Raqchi, south of Cusco and suffered the indignity of its inhabitants, who refused to hear him and cast him out, throwing stones. Viracocha retaliated by raining fire on Raqchi, burning all the people and continued northwest and reached what is today Cusco, then continued along a straight path until the sea near Tumbes (northern Peru, near the Ecuador border.) On those beaches were waiting for him his disciples, and Viracocha walked on the water, and walked away with his followers in the immensity of the ocean. (33) The latter again is most likely a Catholic corruption of earlier oral traditions which state that he departed on a raft or ship of snakes.

The actual name Viracocha was said by some to have been conferred later, when he disappeared on the sea near Tumbes (Vira, fermentation; cocha, body of water), and he perhaps during the journey did not have a name we know of now.

4: The Path Of Viracocha

The scholar of Andean mythology. Maria Scholten de D'Ebneth (1926 to 2007), expressed, in his book "The route of Viracocha" (1977) that, during his trip, Viracocha started the foundation for future cities, which were expanded upon later. Could the foundations referred to be the megalithic works that were later added onto, and adjacently but such cultures as the Inca? Scholten (who based his research on the book of 1613 "Relacion de antiguedades deste reino del Peru", and whose author was Santa Cruz Pachacutic Yamqui Salcamayhua), verified that Tiwanaku, Copacabana, Pukara, Raqchi, Cusco (Sachsayhuaman), Ollantaytambo, Machu Pic'chu, Vitcos and Cajamarca are all archaeological sites "aligned" according to the path followed by Viracocha, from Tiwanaku to Tumbes. (34) All of the above places also contain megalithic works whose construction methods conventional academics cannot account for.

Was Viracocha/Tunupa an ethereal creator or flesh and blood? That will never be known for sure. What could be, is that rather than one or the other, Viracocha may have been the deity of creation, and Viracochan his living representative, moving along a northwest path that we know of as the "path of Viracocha." (35) The road itself which connects these sites is not a straight line per se; taking into account the rugged highland terrain of the Andes, a straight southeast to northwest path would be impossible. However, the Inca road system does travel through many of the sacred sites of the "path of Viracocha" and this will be addressed next.

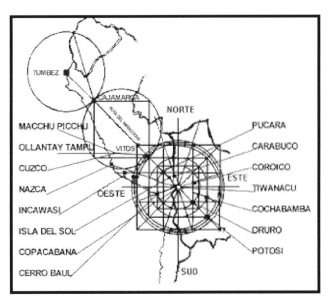

Diagram of the "path of Viracocha"

The Inca road system was the most extensive and advanced transportation system in pre-Columbian South America. (36) The construction of the roads required a large expenditure of time and effort, and the quality of that construction is borne out by the fact that it is still in quite good condition after over 400 years of use since the end of the Inca. The network was based on two north-south roads with numerous branches. The eastern route ran high in the puna grasslands and Andes mountain valleys from Quito, Ecuador to Mendoza, Argentina. It is northwest to southeast in plan and execution, like the "path of Viracocha." The western route followed the coastal plain including in coastal deserts where it hugged the foothills. (37)

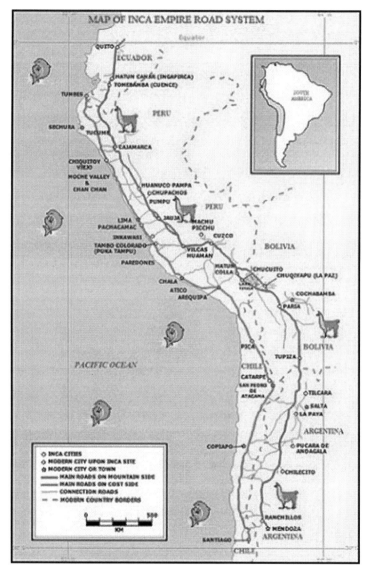

Map of the Inca road system

More than twenty routes ran over the western mountains, while others traversed the eastern cordillera in the mountains and lowlands. Some of these roads reach heights of over 5,000 metres (16,000 ft) above sea level. The trails connected the regions of the Inca world from the northern provincial capital in Quito, Ecuador past the modern city of Santiago, Chile in the south.

Part of the royal Inca road at high elevation

The Inca road system linked together about 40,000 kilometres (25,000 mi) of roadway and provided access to over 3,000,000 square kilometres (1,200,000 sq mi) of territory. (38) Situated between 500 to 800 metres (1,600 to 2,600 ft) above sea level, this monumental road, which could reach 20 metres (66 ft) in width, connected populated areas, administrative centres, agricultural and mining zones as well as ceremonial centres and sacred spaces. Much of the system was the result of the Incas claiming exclusive right over numerous traditional routes, some of which had been constructed centuries earlier mostly by the Wari Empire. Many new sections were built or upgraded substantially: through Chile's Atacama Desert, and along the western margin of Lake Titicaca, serve as two examples. (39)
The Qhapaq Nan (English: *Great Inca Road*, or *Main Andean Road*, and meaning "the beautiful road") constituted the principal north-south highway of the Inca Empire travelling 6,000 kilometres (3,700 mi) along the spine of the Andes, corresponding in position and orientation with the "path of Viracocha." The Qhapaq Nan unified this immense and heterogeneous civilization through a well-organized political system of power. It allowed the Inca to control the confederation and to send troops as needed from the capital, Cusco. (40)

As has been discussed, the Inca did not build the entire road system attributed to them, but developed an efficient network based on expanding and improving earlier roads made by such cultures as the Wari. The Wari civilization was a political formation that emerged around AD 600 in the central highlands of Peru and lasted for about 500 years, to 1100 AD. It operated about the same time as the Tiwanaku culture and at one time was thought to have been derived from it.

In 2008 archaeologists found a prehistoric city, the Northern Wari ruins, also called Cerro Patapo, near modern Chiclayo. The find was the first to show an extensive settlement related to the Wari culture that far north and demonstrate that they had a long span of influence. (41) Construction of an extensive network of roadways linking provincial cities, as well as the construction of complex, characteristic architecture in its major centres, some of which were quite extensive lead many scholars to believe that the Wari were an empire, or closely knit confederation of states. Leaders had to plan projects and organize large amounts of labour to accomplish such projects. (42)

Royal Wari road just south of Cusco

When expanding to engulf new polities, the Wari practised a policy of allowing the local leaders of the newly acquired territory to retain control of their area if they agreed to join and obey the Wari. The Wari required mit'a labour (non-reciprocal public labour for the state) of its subjects as a form of tribute. Mit'a labourers were involved in the construction of buildings at the Wari capital and in the provinces, as well as the roadway system no doubt. Such a practice was adopted and expanded on by the Inca once they took over the Wari territories.

As a result of centuries of drought, the Wari culture began to deteriorate around 800 A.D. Archeologists have determined that the city of Wari (or Huari, near Ayacucho) was dramatically depopulated by 1000 A.D., although it continued to be occupied by a small number of descendant groups. Buildings in Wari and in other government centres had doorways that were deliberately blocked up, as if the Wari intended to return, someday when the rains returned. (43)

The rise of the Inca coincided more or less with the demise of the Wari. Archaeological evidence shows significant levels of inter-personal violence, suggesting that warfare and raiding increased amongst rival groups upon the collapse of the Wari state structure. The Inca themselves were believed to have been forced out of their home territory, in the Lake Titicaca region, and most likely the islands of the Moon and Sun in present day Bolivia as the result of the same drought situation plaguing the Wari further north. Or, they may have been the last of the rulers of Tiwanaku, which, also suffering from drought was attacked by local Aymara tribal people about the year 1000 AD. (44)

The Tiwanaku culture expanded southwards, most likely during the height of their power and influence somewhere between 600 and 800 AD. Part of the reason for such growth may have been able to access the silver rich mines in Potosi, later taken advantage of by the Inca, and ruthlessly exploited by the colonial Spanish after the fall of the Inca. The roads used may have actually preceded the Tiwanaku, since Potosi, being literally a mountain of silver would have been utilized by any culture prior to that time.

Early map of Potosi

5: Below The Path Of Viracocha: Chile

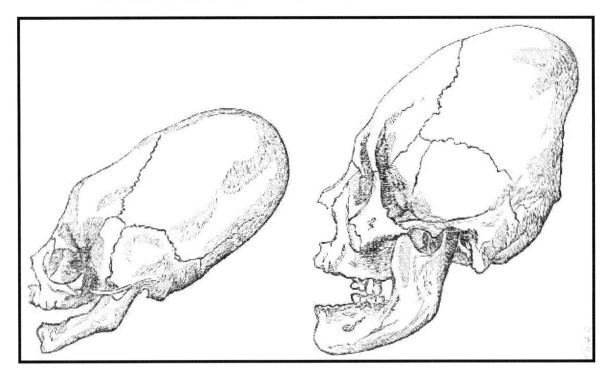

Classic elongated skulls of Peru

We now turn to looking at the elongated skulls and their locations, starting south and moving north. We will find a very interesting correlation between where they have been found in relation to the "path of Viracocha." We will see that very little if any radiocarbon testing has been done on the skulls, and that presumptions of their ages is based on scant actual scientific data. Therefore, I have chosen the "path of Viracocha" to at least show that there is a pattern as to where the elongated skulls are found.

Though some elongated skulls, most likely the result of ACD have been cited in Argentina, the sites farthest south with elongated skulls in any appreciable numbers having been found are in the coastal area of Arica, Chile, close to the Peru border. This practice occurred for a period of at least 5,000 years in the region of Arica and applied both maritime hunter-gatherer groups of the Chinchorro Culture in the Archaic period, and fishermen groups and the Early agroalfareros periods, Early Intermediate, Middle (Tiwanaku Culture) and Late Intermediate or Regional Development. (46)

The earliest sites (mostly middens) of the Chinchorro date as early as 7,000 BC at the site of Acha. The first evidence of mummification dates to approximately 5,000 BC, in the Quebrada de Camarones region, making the Chinchorro mummies the oldest in the world. (47) This process, and the culture itself seems to have ended at about 1800

BC, and so this means that at least some of the Chinchorro elongated skulls go back to at least that date, if not earlier, and perhaps much earlier at that. What this tells us is that as a culture, the Chinchorro were practising ACD before any other in South America, as far as is known.

But if this is the case, why? The Chinchorro were a technologically, and one would presume culturally simple Stone Age people, whose main food resource was the ocean. Although only a handful of settlement sites have been identified to date, Chinchorro communities were likely small groups of huts housing single nuclear families, with a population size of approximately 30 to 50 individuals. Large shell middens were found by Junius Bird in the 1940s, adjacent to the huts at the site of Acha in Chile.

The Quiana 9 site, dated to 4420 BC, contained the remains of several semicircular huts located on the slope of an Arica coastal hill. The huts there were built of posts with sea mammal skin roofs. Caleta Huelen 42, near the mouth of the Loa River in Chile, had several semi-subterranean circular huts with superimposed floors, implying long-term ongoing settlement. (48) The Chinchorro were also found as south as the Iquique area, approximately 220 km south of Arica. In the Museo Regional de Iquique are found several elongated skulls on display from the Chinchorro. Their genetic origins have not been determined, nor reasons why they performed ACD or where the cultural practise came from.

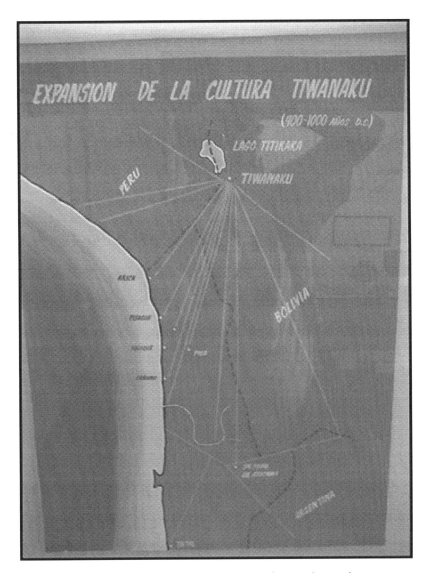

Map of southern influence by Tiwanaku culture

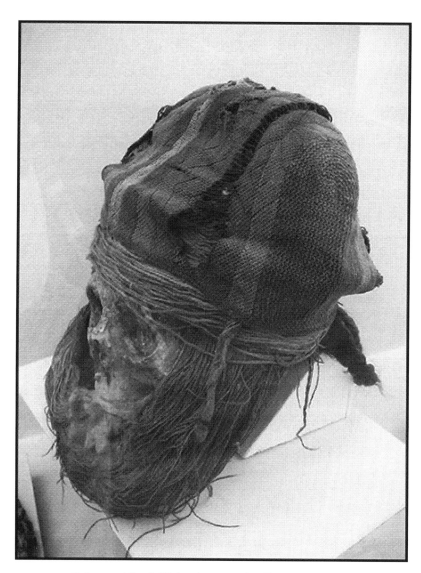

Mummified Chinchorro skull with textile

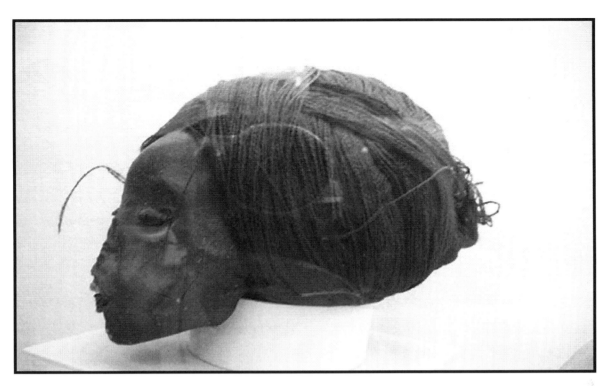

Chinchorro mummy skull with braided hair

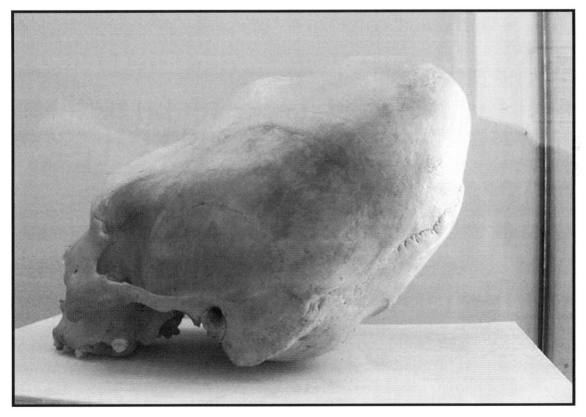

Chinchorro area skull similar to Tiwanaku

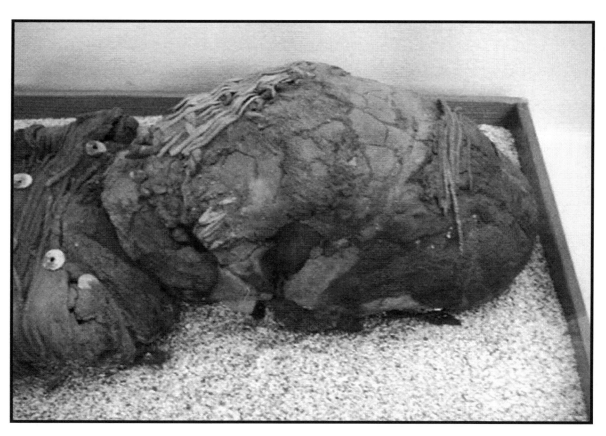

Classic Chinchorro mummified skull

6: Tunupa and Uyuni

Volcan Tunupa rising above the Uyuni salt flats

If we travel to the east, and slightly south, we find our next major area of interest, Volcan Tunupa, which rises to a height of 5432 meters from the salt flats of Uyuni, which are the largest in the world. The volcano is of course named after Tunupa, the creator deity of the Aymara people and in a cave just above the village of Coquesa are located 6 mummies with elongated skulls. Estimates vary widely as to their age, from 1000 to 3000 years, but since radiocarbon testing has not been performed, and no archaeological work has been done here, more precise data is not available. The author's visit there in November of 2013 allowed him to assess that the ACD was of a rather crude nature. When local people are asked what culture they represent, the overwhelming answer is simply "Aymara," however, no proper archaeological study of this immediate area has been made.

Elongated skull inside a cave at Volcan Tunupa

Southeast of Volcan Tunupa by 120 km is the mining town of Uyuni, and there we find the Museo Arqueologico y Antropologico de los Andes Meridionales. This museum has a small collection of elongated skulls showing what would appear to be typical ACD, as can be seen in the photos.

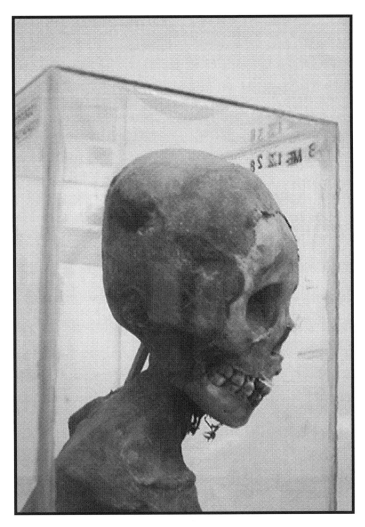

Mummified skeleton from Uyuni

Once again, the museum literature states that the elongated skulls are from the Aymara culture, who date back perhaps 900 to 1000 years, though some estimates, largely unsubstantiated by scientific data, push their history back a further 4000 years. It is more likely that prior to 1000 years ago, the Aymara ancestors were comprised of different small groupings of people that later coalesced. If the skulls from both Uyuni and Volcan Tunupa are of Aymara origin, they could of course be related, and in fact the Uyuni museum ones could in fact have come from the Tunupa area.

7: Potosi

If we move next northeast by 120 km we reach the city of Potosi, home to one of the greatest silver mines in the world. In the pre-Hispanic period, Potosi was only a small hamlet perched at an altitude of 4,000 m, in the icy solitude of the Andes. It owes its prosperity to the discovery, between 1542 and 1545, of the New World's biggest silver lodes in the Cerro de Potosi, the mountain south of the city which overlooks it. As a result, Potosi is directly and tangibly associated with an event of outstanding universal significance: the economic change brought about in the 16th century by the flood of Spanish currency resulting from the massive import of precious metals from the New World into Seville. (49)

Potosi was used by the Inca, but was not exploited in the way the Spanish colonials turned it into a strip mine, which resulted in the deaths of hundreds of thousands of Native workers. In the centre of the city of Potosi is the Casa de la Monedas, originally the official mint, and then converted into a museum.

Inside this imposing yet beautifully restored colonial Spanish building are a few elongated skulls. One would presume they are from the area, but there is scant information in the museum as regards how old the skulls are, or where they were found.

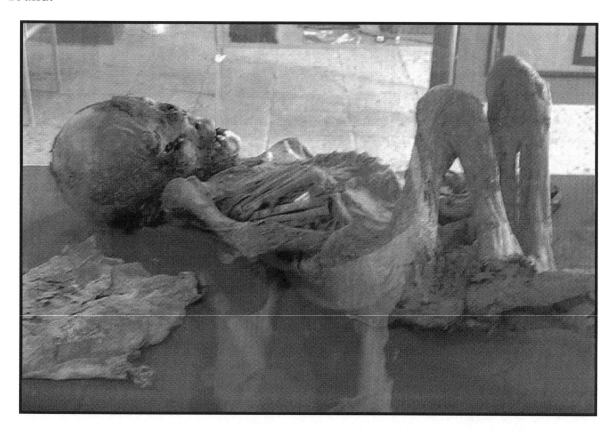

Mummified child with elongated skull in Potosi museum

8: Oruro

Next, we move northwest by approximately 210 km and reach the city of Oruro. Here, far off in one corner of the city we find the Museo Nacional Antropologico Eduardo Lopez Rivas. The museum was founded on 1 November 1959 and has four areas: Archaeology, Ethnomusicology, Ethnography and Folklore. It has a large collection of elongated skulls on display, most being stated as being from the Wankarani culture. The Wankarani people lived in the central Altiplano of the south-central Andes during the Formative period (2000 BC-AD 400) according to some sources, while others suggest a narrower period of 1200 BC to 100 AD.

The austere environment of the south central Andes appears to be a formidable place to live, but the Wankarani people are a testament to the capacity for human adaptation to the elements. They employed a successful subsistence strategy and adapted to the harsh environment as agrarian pastorals by exploiting domesticated animals and plants. Archaeological research notes that camelids (such as llama and alpaca) were foundational in their economy both as a source of food and an icon of ritual culture. Researchers cite stone tool technologies such as stone hoes as evidence of agricultural activity, and conclude these data indicate that the Wankarani farmed quinoa and potatoes. (50)

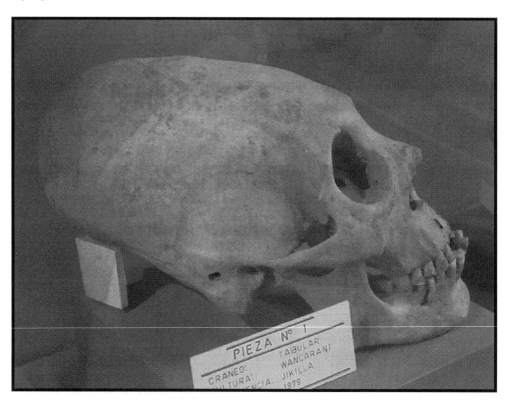

Tabular Wankarani skull

They were makers of somewhat crude but useful ceramics, with geometric and animal symbols, were smelting copper and possibly bronze to a limited extent, and are believed to have been absorbed into the Tiwanaku culture. This is evidenced by the presence of Tiwanaku ceramics in some Wankarani sites.

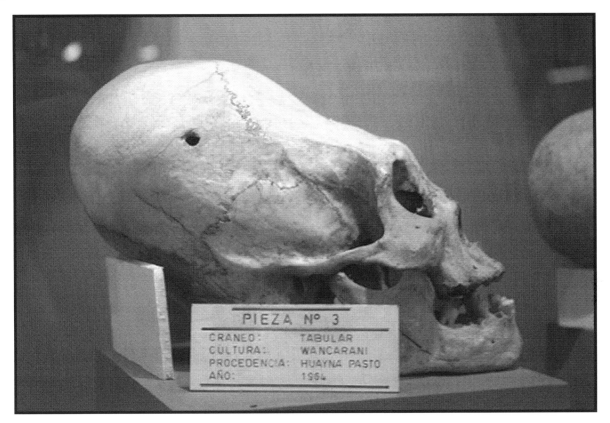

Another amazing Wankarani skull

9: Tiwanaku and Puma Punku

The famous Sun Gate at Tiwanaku

And it is off to Tiwanaku that we will explore next, about 200 km northwest of Oruro. Tiwanaku is recognized by Andean scholars as one of the most important civilizations prior to the Inca Empire; it was the ritual and administrative capital of a major state power for approximately five hundred years. The area around Tiwanaku may have been inhabited as early as 1500 BC as a small agricultural village. (51) Most research has studied the Tiwanaku IV and V periods between AD 300 and AD 1000, during which the polity grew significantly in power. During the time period between 300 BC and AD 300, Tiwanaku is thought to have been a moral and cosmological centre to which many people made pilgrimages. Researchers believe it achieved this standing prior to expanding its powerful empire. (52)

Around AD 400 a state in the Titicaca basin began to develop and an urban capital was built at Tiwanaku. It expanded its reaches and brought its culture and way of life to many other cultures in Peru, Bolivia, and the people of the northern regions of Argentina and Chile. And it was not exclusively a military or violent culture. In order to expand its reach, Tiwanaku used politics to create colonies, negotiate trade agreements (which made the other cultures rather dependent), and establish state cults. (53) Others were drawn into the Tiwanaku civilization due to religious beliefs, as it continued as a religious center. Force was rarely necessary for the empire to expand, but on the northern end of the basin, resistance was present. There is evidence that bases of some statues were taken from other cultures and carried all the way back to the capital city of Tiwanaku, where the stones were placed in a subordinate position to the deities of the Tiwanaku. Of the sculptures that remain, most are believed to be depictions of Viracocha, including one that is the Bennett Monolith. The Bennett Monolith is of 7.3 meters high and has an approximate weight of 20 tons. It is the biggest Andean statue known of.

Discovered at Tiwanaku in 1932 by archaeologist Wendell C. Bennett, later in the 1930s it was moved from Tiwanaku to the city of La Paz, to be placed in an open museum in the Tejada Serrano Square, where it stayed until 2001 before being finally moved to the new museum of stone objects at Tiwanaku itself.

Figure 113. The Gigantic Idol in the trench. This idol, according to the still current popular tradition, was "Pachamama," goddess of the Food-giving Earth. This is the state in which it was found, when it was completely excavated by the author and placed on cross-ties to be taken to La Paz.

Photo of Viracocha sculpture being unearthed

(54) The amazing thing is that both this statue, along with a shorter 2+ meters high were found buried in what is called the Subterranean Temple. Both are purported to

be depictions of Viracocha, and the smaller one has an obvious moustache and beard, facial characteristics not typical of modern, and one would assume ancient Andean Native people.

The community grew to urban proportions between AD 600 and AD 800, becoming an important regional power in the southern Andes. Early estimates figured that the city had covered approximately 6.5 square kilometers at its maximum, with between 15,000 and 30,000 inhabitants. However, satellite imaging since the late 20th century has caused researchers to dramatically raise their estimates of population. They found that the extent of fossilized suka kollus (raised agricultural terraces) across the three primary valleys of Tiwanaku appeared to have the capacity to support a population of between 285,000 and 1,482,000 people. (55) The elites' power continued to grow along with the surplus of resources until about AD 950. At this time a dramatic shift in climate occurred, as is typical for the region.

Author David Hatcher Childress and bearded Viracocha

A significant drop in precipitation occurred in the Titicaca Basin, and some archaeologists suggest a great drought occurred. As the rain was reduced, many of the cities furthest away from Lake Titicaca began to produce fewer crops to give to those in power. As the surplus of food dropped, the elites' power began to fall. Due to the resiliency of the raised fields, the capital city became the last place of agricultural production. With continued drought, people died or moved elsewhere. Tiwanaku disappeared around 1000 AD,(56) and the land was not inhabited again for many years, until the arrival of the Aymara, perhaps about 1100 AD, or, in fact, it may have been Aymara speaking people who chased the last of the Tiwanaku people out. Many scholars believe that the Inca originated in this immediate area, and/or the Islands of the Sun and Moon in Lake Titicaca, and were driven north towards Cusco by the Aymara.

The enigmatic place called Tiwanaku, and Puma Punku, which is designated as a separate site than that of Tiwanaku but in close geographic proximity have interesting characteristics that conventional archaeology has not, and to some degree perhaps does not, want to cover. And those are, the finding of many elongated skulls in the immediate area, and the astonishing level of stone shaping technology that apparently existed at these sites in ancient times. The main museum at Tiwanaku had elongated skulls on display as late as 2008 (57) but the author, having first visited the area at about that time saw nothing but a papered over display. On subsequent visits since then, at least 10 in number, the case remained empty and camouflaged with paper. Upon enquiring why the display was closed on the first few visits, the staff claimed they were "cleaning the skulls." However, as this "cleaning" process dragged on over the years, they basically stated that the display was closed, permanently.

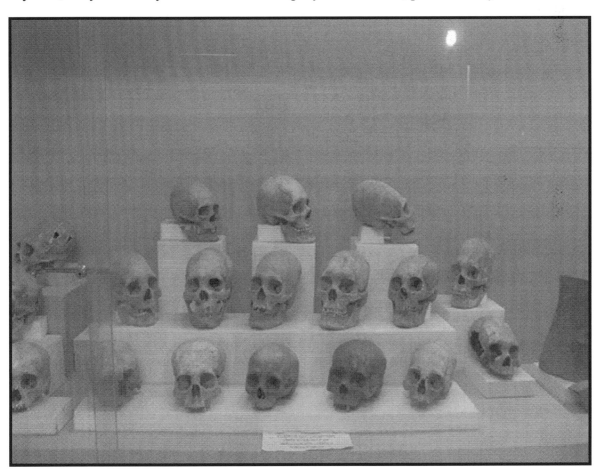

Former display case at the Tiwanaku Museum in Tiwanaku

Now why would this be? Clearly the skulls represented an important part of the museum display, as it showed who actual lived in, and presumably built Tiwanaku and Puma Punku. And there is scant information to be gleaned from academic sources on this subject. Most internet information speculates wildly that the elongated skulls represent aliens, or the remnants of descendants of Atlantis. However, one in depth analysis of the presence of ACD during the Tiwanaku period indicates that such a high percentage of specimens analyzed were cranially deformed that it unlikely represented a special social class or classes. (58)

Another paper, based on analysis of elongated skulls and Tiwanaku style pottery found in the Moquegua Valley of southern Peru would seem to indicate that ACD found in that area was a direct result of the expansion of the Tiwanaku culture. Moquegua's elevation (1200 meters) and temperate climate made this region highly valuable to highland Tiwanaku, whose region was and is relatively low yielding as regards agriculture. Also, Moquegua's strategic position on routes to coastal resources and local deposits of copper no doubt added to its worth to Tiwanaku, some 300 km away. (59) The report goes on to say that elongated skulls found in northern Chile, such as those in the Tarapaca region (in between Iquique on the coast, and Volcan Tunupa) could be from immigrants from Tiwanaku. And, the elongated skulls found in the Arica area of northern Chile may also be of Tiwanaku origin, rather than being from the Chinchorro. If this is the case, then it is possible that most of the elongated skulls found from the northern coast of Chile east to Potosi and north to Tiwanaku belong to the Tiwanaku culture of approximately 100 to 1000 AD, except the Wankarani, who most reports believe to have existed from about 1200 BC to 100 AD. Could the Wankarani be the first people of the area to have performed ACD, and created the process? There is too scant information to make such a presumption.

Child skeleton no longer on display at Tiwanaku Museum in La Paz

To the author's knowledge, actual radiocarbon testing has not been performed on the elongated skulls found at Puma Punku or Tiwanaku, and thus their actual age has most likely not been established. Conventional archaeology assumes them to be contemporary with the construction phases at Tiwanaku, and thus about 100 to 1000 AD. However, it is also the quality of the stone work itself which has not been adequately explained to the satisfaction of many; especially those that have actually been there in person.

There are two main types of stone to be found at Puma Punku and Tiwanaku, namely red sandstone and grey andesite. A third may be grey sandstone, in the form of monoliths at the Kalasasaya complex at Tiwanaku.

The author and single piece of red sandstone

The red sandstone used in this site's structures has been determined by petrographic analysis to come from a quarry 10 kilometers away and on top of a mountain; a remarkable distance considering that the largest of these stones that still remain, as the Tiwanaku structures were used as quarries by later people up until the 20th century, which is at Puma Punku weighs 131 metric tons. (60) The grey andesite stones that were used to create the most elaborate shapes and monoliths originate from the Copacabana peninsula, located north, on Lake Titicaca and some 70 kilometers away. One theory is that these giant andesite stones, which weigh over 40 tons, were transported some 90 kilometers across Lake Titicaca on reed boats, then laboriously dragged another 10 kilometers to the city. (61)

This idea is simply ludicrous, and to the author's knowledge has never been tested in the field, even with scale models. To confound this primitive idea even more, local experts believe that the andesite quarry is presently under the waters of Lake Titicaca, and presumably has been so for considerable time. It is also the precise nature of the flatness of the surfaces, as well as the fact that the area is more or less above the tree line, that make such a concept unfeasible. How would you drag a 40 ton block across relatively damp terrain without wooden rollers of some kind? And if academics believe that cylindrical stones were used, what level of technology would be required to make them more or less perfectly round?

What intrigues visitors to Tiwanaku and Puma Punku, but especially the latter if they have the sense to closely inspect the andesite surfaces is how flat they are. The vast majority of tour guides insist that the Tiwanaku culture was responsible for these achievements, and drawings of the stone shaping process adorn the inner walls of the local onsite museum. What they depict are Native men with pony tails, and wearing scant clothing pounding the andesite with simple stone hammers.

One of many flat surfaces at Tiwanaku and Puma Punku

Any engineer that the author has escorted to the site, of which there have been many scoff at such an idea. Christopher Dunn, a master machinist of British birth, but living in the United States, has measured the flatness of the surfaces at Puma Punku on more than one occasion, and once with the author. He has calculated that some of the surfaces are within some 10,000ths of an inch from being laser straight; a feat that could not have been done with hand tools; especially those of the Bronze Age Tiwanaku culture. As well, drill holes of uniform size are found in many of the blocks, and the ancient builders, whoever they were, preferred the use of precise angles other than 90 degrees in most cases in the stone.

The ancient builders were not fond of 90 degree angles

Carbon dates extrapolated from organic artifacts buried about the stone megalithic structures give ranges of anywhere from 1500 BC to around 400 AD for the original foundation of the Tiwanaku site. The total area that has been excavated thus far of the site though is just less than 2%, which consists of many cross contaminated layers, that is to say layers of age, older and newer, that intermix and therefore provide no accurate basis upon which the true date of each individual strata can be evaluated along with subsequent finds. For example, sample P-123 was found and dated to just 133 AD but was found at levels of which primarily artifacts of the oldest layer, c. 1500 BC, were thought to reside. From the evidence it would seem that the common system of contextualizing different layers most often used in archaeological practices is unreliable within the particular layers of Tiwanaku, random and unpredictable as they are in analyzing the given age of certain artifacts. (62)

Also notable is the fact that archaeologists working in Tiwanaku and Puma Punku have uncovered materials only 3.75 meters below ground and concluded, on the basis of digging only a mere 75 cm beyond 4 m, that no prior signs of human occupation could be found lower than the prescribed 4 meter mark.

Andesite slabs still partially buried in mud

Any visitor to the area can see that not only has there been extreme looting of the stone for at least 1000 years, perhaps from the first arrival of the Aymara people, but much of Puma Punku and Tiwanaku appear to be buried in thick red mud. Proof of much earlier occupations has already been established by ground penetrating radar, magnetometry, induced electrical conductivity, and magnetic susceptibility. All of which point to structures, buildings and compounds, water conduits, residential compounds, and widespread gravel pavements all hidden underneath the ground going from the Kalasasaya compound in Tiwanaku, all the way to Puma Punku. At such a depth it suggests a very old date for the oldest parts of the ruins. Sufficient water or wind erosion would not be present on the dry arid expanse of the Bolivian highlands to cover the stones at such a depth without a significant elapse in geological time. In addition, Puma Punku shows significant signs of flood damage, and major mud and sand deposits many meters thick over the stone work, some blocks scattered about and pushed against embankments as if by some massive flood and earthquakes. (63)

The Altiplano area where Tiwanaku and Puma Punku are located was covered in a giant inland sea known as Lake Tauca which lasted from 16,000 to around 13,000BC. As the above sites are elevated above the surrounding area, they may have been above these waters at that time. Then there may have been a dry spell when the Altiplano would have been covered in fertile mud until around 11,000BC when the Altiplano was covered by the shallower lake Coipasa which lasted a further 1500 years.

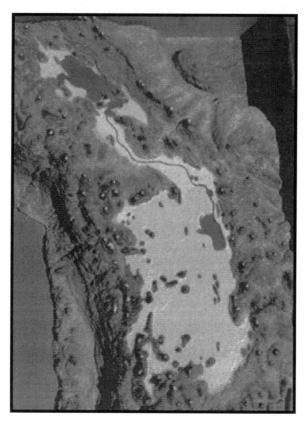

Map of how Lake Titicaca looked more than 10,000 years ago

Evidence of this flooding was also found by Bolivian archaeologist Arthur Posnansky, who documented that at one time the lakes above Lake Titicaca flooded to bursting point, the waters poured down into Lake Titicaca causing that lake to flood and drown the city of Tiwanaku. The waters then continued south along the Altiplano which according to Posnansky also sank in elevation, leaving the sloping strand line of the former lakes. (64)

The author measuring a large displaced andesite slab at Tiwanaku

Arthur Posnansky (1873 to 1946), often called "Arturo", was at various times in his life an engineer, explorer, ship's navigator, director of a river navigation company, entrepreneur, La Paz city council member, and well known and well respected avocational archaeologist. Though born in Vienna, Austria, he immigrated to South America in 1896 and finally settled in Bolivia, where he was intrigued by the ancient sites around Lake Titicaca. The results of these investigations were published in books such as *The Islands of Titicaca and Koati* and *Rasas y monumentos prehistoricos Del Altiplano Andino*. For such research, the Bolivian Senate awarded him a gold medal in 1905 and he later became Director of the National Museum. He also authored books, which included *Os Indios Paumaris e Ipurinas no Rio Purus* (1898) and *Mapa del Rio Acre* (7 volumes, 1897), about South American geography and ethnology. He also lectured about archaeological subjects in Berlin, Frankfort, Nuremberg, and Treptow, Germany. In recognition of his accomplishments, the German Government conferred on him an honorary title of Professor in 1914. (65)

In 1945 (volumes I and II) and 1957 (volumes III and IV), Posnansky's final and most important book, *Tihuanacu, the Cradle of American Man,* was published. In it, Posnansky argued that Tiwanaku was constructed approximately 17,000 years ago by American peoples, although not by the ancestors of those then living in the area, the Aymara. Posnansky also saw Tiwanaku as the origin point of civilization throughout the Americas, including the Inca, the Maya and others. (66) He explains his theories, which are rooted in archeoastronomy, as follows. Since Earth is tilted on its axis in respect to the plane of the solar system, the resulting angle is known as the "obliqueness of the ecliptic" (one should not confuse this with another astronomical phenomenon known as "Precession", as critics of Posnansky have done). If viewed from the earth, the planets of our solar system travel across the sky in a line called the *plane of the ecliptic*.

At present our earth is tilted at an angle to of 23 degrees and 27 minutes, but this angle is not constant. The angle oscillates slowly between 22 degrees and 1 minute minimum to an extreme of 24 degrees and 5 minutes. A complete cycle takes roughly 41,000 years to complete. The alignment of the Kalasasaya temple depicts a tilt of the earth's axis amounting to 23 degrees, 8 minutes, 48 seconds, which according to astronomers, indicates a date of 15,000 B.C.

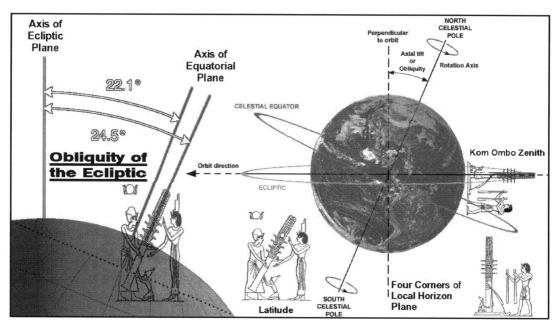

Diagram of the Obliquity of the Ecliptic

Between 1927 and 1930 Prof. Posnansky's conclusions were studied intensively by a number of authorities. Dr. Hans Ludendorff (Director of the Astronomical Observatory of Potsdam), Friedrich Becker of the Specula Vaticana, Prof. Arnold Kohlschutter (astronomer at Bonn University), and Rolf Müller (astronomer of the Institute of Astrophysics at Potsdam) verified the accuracy of Posnansky's calculations and vouched for the reliability of his conclusions. (67)

The elongated skulls found at Tiwanaku and Puma Punku were extracted from the cross contaminated layers of the excavations, and has been previously stated there are no published reports of any radiocarbon dating of them. The red mud of the area would be an almost perfect preservation material, and thus simple visual examination would not determine how long they had been interred.

However, just outside the main fencing of Puma Punku there is a restaurant, and the owner has done excavations in the area in order to construct foundations for a building. In the soil taken out he found many human bones, as well as some elongated skulls. The pottery found in these deposits are of the Tiwanaku culture, and are thus up to 2000 years old, with a minimum dating of 1000 years. It is circumstantial of course, but one can conclude that these skulls were from Tiwanaku people.

On a recent visit, as in December of 2014 the author was shocked to find a new display of elongated skulls in the main museum at Tiwanaku. Thanks to the director of the site, we were allowed to fly a quad copter equipped with a high definition video camera over all of Tiwanaku and Bolivia, as well as photographing the new skull display.

Large elongated skull outside restaurant near Puma Punku

What you can see from the photos below is that this rather innovative display shows attempts at facial reconstruction of some of the skulls, including an infant. The facial features, if these reconstructions can be trusted for accuracy, are not similar to the local resident population, possibly indicating that whoever the Tiwanaku people were, they were strikingly different than the Aymara.

According to the chronicles of one of the first of the Spanish conquistadors to venture into this area in the early 1600s, Garcia de la Vega asked the Inca residents of Tiwanaku at that time if they had built the stone structures.

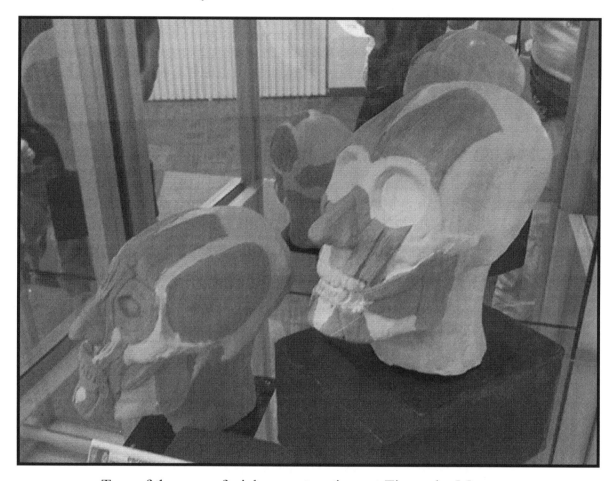

Two of the many facial reconstructions at Tiwanaku Museum

The response was laughter, followed by statements that it was the Viracochas who had done the work, thousands of years before the Inca existed.

23 km due north of Tiwanaku and Puma Punku, in the area of Patapatani Bolivia is a site called *Torres Funerarias de Taramaya*. Here are 6 funeral towers, locally known as Chullpa, made of local field stone and mud/clay mortar, with the tallest being approximately 3 metres. Inside of these some skeletons with elongated skulls were found.

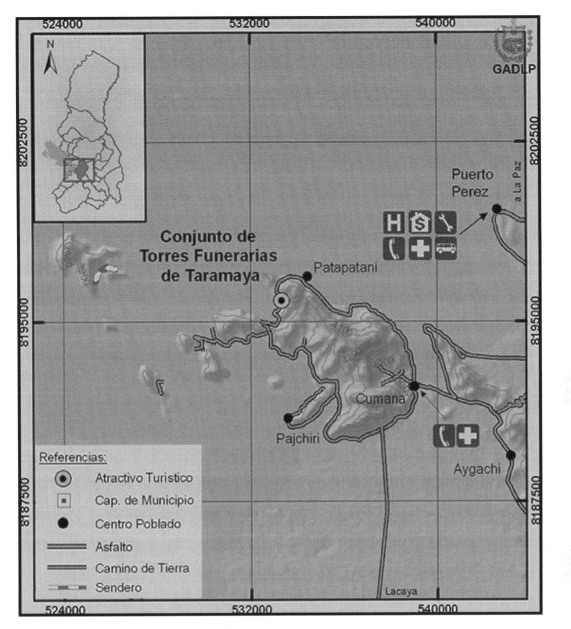

Map of the Taramaya area

There is scant information about this site, aside from it clearly being pre-Colombian, however, archaeology digs in the area have gleaned Tiwanaku period ceramics.

10: Island Of The Sun

Approximately 50 km northwest of Taramaya is the Island of the Sun, thought by many scholars to have been the homeland of the Inca prior to their establishment of Cusco. It was here that the Inca creation story began by most accounts. In the beginning, all was darkness and nothing existed. Viracocha the Creator came forth from the waters of Lake Titicaca and created the land and the sky before returning to the lake. He also created a race of people in some versions of the story they were giants. These people and their leaders displeased Viracocha, as has been previously stated, so he came out of the lake again and flooded the world to destroy them. He also turned some of the men into stones. Then Viracocha created the Sun, Moon and stars. (68) Interestingly, these oral traditions do somewhat concur with the evidence of a catastrophic mud flow event at Tiwanaku and Puma Punku, as previously stated, that may have occurred more than 10,000 years ago.

Most mythology does contain at least grains of truth about the actual history of people and their area, although the poetic nature of oral traditions tends to heavily water down most of the facts. The idea of the flood myth stated above does have its roots in actual geologic data, since as was previously stated Lake Titicaca was at one time much larger than it is today, and Tiwanaku and Puma Punku may have been victims of a massive inundation of water several thousand years ago.

Inca ruins on the Island of the Sun

Going back to the creation story, then Viracocha made men to populate the different areas and regions of the world. He created people, but left them inside the Earth. The Inca referred to the first men as *Vari Viracocharuna*. Viracocha then created another group of men, also called *viracochas*. He spoke to these *viracochas* and made them remember the different characteristics of the peoples that would populate the world. Then he sent all of the *viracochas* forth except for two. These *viracochas* went to the caves, streams, rivers and waterfalls of the land, every place where Viracocha had determined that people would come forth from the Earth. The *viracochas* spoke to the people in these places, telling them the time had come for them to come out of the Earth. The people came forth and populated the land. (69)

The Islands of the Sun and Moon are of great significance in Andean prehistory as pilgrimage centres of inter-regional importance and great temporal depth, ultimately gaining their greatest prestige during the Inca civilization. These islands were considered the birthplace of the founders of the Inca lineage in many accounts and were of great consequence in Inca sun worship. The Inca were committed to the islands and built substantial sanctuaries on each. Many of these sites had played a ceremonial role before Inca intervention in the area and were, in fact, associated with earlier states. (70) Tiwanaku pottery has been found on the Island of the Sun and thus showed their presence in the area.

For four months in 1895, Adolph Bandelier conducted research on the Island of the Sun and nearby Island of the Moon as part of a longer research endeavour on behalf of the American Museum of Natural History (AMNH), during which time he acquired a number of the museum's Andean collections. In total, 37 crania were exhumed and all appeared to be those of adults. The sites from which they were excavated ranged in date from the Middle Formative (c. 1300 to 500 BC) through the Altiplano period (c. AD 1100 to 1400.) While only a small sample, these crania are among the few human remains available for study from the Island of the Sun.

Megalithic remnants on the island of the Sun

4 of the 37 showed evidence of trepanation, which is the deliberate removal of bone tissue from the skull by grooving, scraping, drilling, or a combination of these techniques. 2 of these showed no sign of healing, whereas of the other 2, one seemed partially healed and the other completely. And perhaps even more intriguing, all 37 had moderate to pronounced annular modification. The consistency is striking, as is the fact that all the modifications were highly symmetrical, implying some degree of standardization of the practice. The majority of the forms were of the oblique variant (73 percent); the remaining ten crania were erect. Also, there were no significant differences between males and females as regards type of modification.

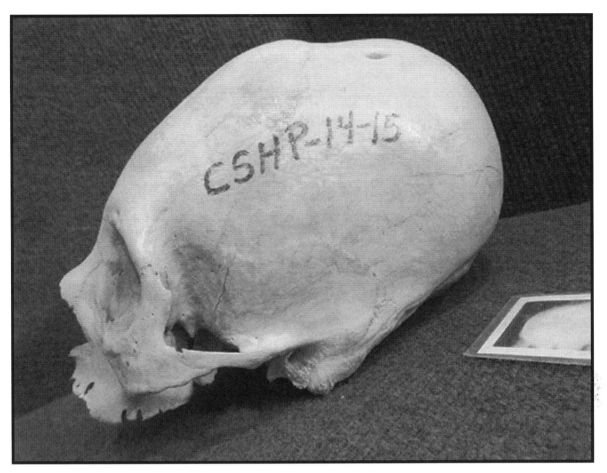
Elongated skull from a tomb near the Island of the Sun

It was not established or recorded what culture or cultures the skulls came from, as ceramic or other artifacts were not referred to, and the sampling was done in 1895 prior to the existence of radiocarbon or DNA testing. One could presume that they range from pre-Tiwanaku through Inca cultures. As an aside, and yet a very important factor, trepanation evidence is very common among the elongated skulls, especially in the Paracas and Inca populations, which will be discussed later.

The author inspecting a baby elongated skull from near the Island of the Sun

11: Sillustani

One of the megalithic Chullpa at Sillustani

Northwest of the Island of the Sun is a major archaeological site called Sillustani, at which elongated skulls have been found in stone funeral structures. The tombs, which are built above ground in tower like structures called *chullpa*, as previously discussed, but far more sophisticated in this area, are the vestiges of the Colla, Aymara speaking people who were conquered by the Inca in the 15th century. The structures housed the remains of complete family groups, although they were probably limited to nobility and unfortunately many of the tombs have been dynamited by grave robbers, while others were left unfinished. (72) The above is the conventional rhetoric espoused by academics, and is the information which most guides to the Sillustani site give visitors. What they generally believe is that the smaller and cruder *chullpa* were created first, by the Colla people between 1200 and 1400 AD and that the Inca, who conquered the Colla during the 15th century constructed the larger and more precise ones afterwards.

Prior to the Colla, the great Tiwanaku civilization held sway to some extent in the area. The Colla, or Hatun Colla was one of many tribes that had organized themselves in communities after the Tiwanaku culture had faded. Together with the Lupaca kingdom the Colla had control over more or less the whole region of Lake Titicaca.

Of course, according to conventional thought, smaller and rougher stone work should precede larger and finer ones, because it is generally believed that humanity has technically evolved over time, whether in Peru or elsewhere. Other works attributed to the Colla in the region are indeed crude in construction and appearance, and made from local field stone which has been roughly shaped and cemented together with clay as mortar.

The cruder chullpa made after the megalithic ones

The finer of the *chullpa* are presumed to be of Inca manufacture, because their form of mortar free construction is compared to such works in Cusco such as the Coricancha. However, it has not been positively proven that the Inca built the Coricancha, and in fact questions arise as to whether or not the Inca, who were a Bronze Age culture could have achieved such fine workmanship.

Megalithic wall of the Coricancha below the church

The Coricancha is thought by many sources, including early Spanish chronicles to be the first building ever constructed by the Inca. However, it is also the finest of their works. So how is this possible? The answer could be that the Coricancha in fact existed in Cusco when the Inca arrived, somewhere between 1000 and 1100 AD, and was made by an unknown earlier people, sometimes referred to as the Perhuas, or indeed Viracochans of whom we have already discussed.

Although this may sound like an outrageous assumption to some readers, anyone who has walked the streets of Cusco can clearly see that the lower and thus older constructions are superior to those that came later. This suggests that the Inca were building, in many cases, on top of older, finer foundations.

The best of the *chullpa* at Sillustani look very much like the Coricancha in Cusco as regards building methods, and materials. Some of the wall areas of the Coricancha are composed of amazingly tight fitting andesite blocks, while others are of basalt. In both cases the stone was not local, but brought on from specific quarries several kilometers away.

It is based on the similarity of appearance alone that have caused many academics to presume that the finest of the Sillustani *chullpa* were made by the Inca. However, if the Coricancha is not Inca, but older, then the *chullpa* may be the same.

Human remains were found inside some of the *chullpa* by archaeologists, and others by tomb robbers. Thus, the conclusion has been drawn that the function of the *chullpa* was of a funerary nature. However, some engineers have looked at these structures, and find the finer ones quite perplexing.

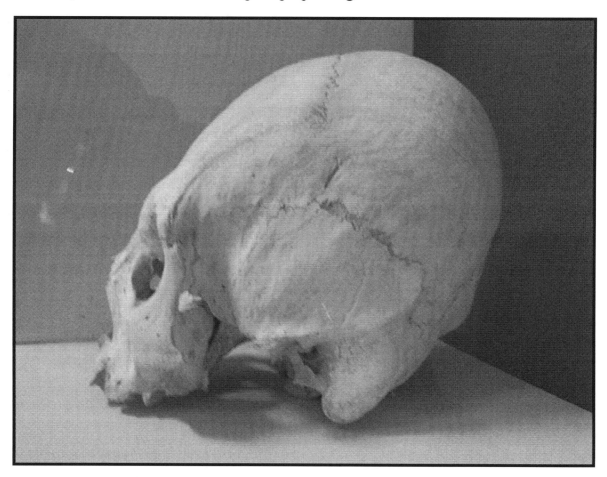

Elongated skull found in one of the Sillustani chullpa

They are not vertically straight, but in fact taper outwards from the bottom to the top, which is not a conventionally logical building approach. Also, the top area has a curve to it from the outside in. As well, each has a band around the upper area which would form what function; simply decoration?

Mortar free construction is clearly far more complex than the use of clay to fill in the areas of the smaller and less well made *chullpa,* or any other building or wall. As well, fitting stones tightly together as is seen in the finer and larger *chullpa* means that the structure is stronger, and could have resonant qualities due to this close stone contact.

The author has been inside one of the best made *chullpa* with engineer Christopher Dunn, author of *The Giza Power Plant* and *Lost Technologies Of Ancient Egypt,* as well as Dr. Robert Schoch, author, geologist, professor and the man who re-dated the Sphinx of Egypt based on water weathering.

In both occasions we noticed that, using a phone application which can emit specific musical notes, "A" and "A#" caused the inside of the *chullpa* to seemingly amplify the sound, while other notes did not. What is curious about this is that some research in the Great Pyramid of Giza's "king's chamber" suggest that it is tuned to "A#".

Now why would a builder supposedly tune the interior of a stone structure to resonate to a particular frequency range? If it was a tomb for the dead, he or she most likely would not, but if it was constructed for an energetic purpose, then it may make sense.

On a trip to the Sillustani site in November of 2013 with Hugh Newman's Megalithomania we had many energy dowsers with us. Clearly not regarded by the mainstream as a scientific testing, these talented individuals were able to pick up specific bands of energy running through areas of the *chullpa.*

The best of the *chullpa* are composed of 2 layers of stone, each being of different composition and from separate quarries. The less finely made and smaller of the *chullpa* have no such organized compositional structure.

Interior of one of the megalithic chullpa

The outer layer of the fine *chullpa* is basalt, and not of local origin, but supposedly from a specific many kilometers away, and the inner "bee hive" dome area is made of dense andesite, again most likely not local, as the Sillustani area is predominantly red sandstone. Also, in those of the fine *chullpa* which are somewhat intact, the stones of the inner andesite core are cemented together with a white clay material which again is not of local origin.

The *chullpa* of smaller size and inferior quality are made of field stone and broken pieces of red sandstone, basalt and andesite, with red adobe material, which is in fact the soil of the area, used as filler and binding agent.

Another curious aspect to the *chullpa* in general is that each has a small opening at the base, facing east. This cardinal alignment is speculated by most archaeologists as being related to the path of the sun, which rises in the east and sets in the west. Since the Inca, and presumably earlier people were "sun worshippers" these archaeologists believe that east facing "door" relates to the religious belief system of these people, and that as a tomb each *chullpa* may guide the departed soul to some kind of solar related afterlife.

However, the damage to all of the finer *chullpa,* believed by many to have been the result of looting and stone material recycling centuries ago, is greatest on the western sides of these towers. If it is possible that rather than originally being graves of nobility, they were in fact energetic structures of some kind, some engineers have speculated that an ancient catastrophic event, such as a power overload or earthquake may have caused the original damage.

Remains of a large square chullpa

In fact, the largest of the *chullpa,* which was square in shape and composed of several multi-ton blocks, is the best case to approach this idea. Some of the megalithic stones which were originally incorporated into its from are to be found several hundred feet away, hardly something that people wishing to harvest material would do.

In summary, the main points are the following. It is quite possible that the oldest of the *chullpa,* which are of the finest craftsmanship and design predate the Bronze Age

Inca or any other known culture. The later, smaller and poorer quality structures were an attempt by later cultures to copy the design, and to use the older *chullpa,* which no longer had an energetic function due to damage, as funerary depositories. The fact that the elongated skulls have not been specifically described as to in which *chullpa* they were found makes it impossible to date them. Also, at Sillustani as is the case in all of the sites that have been explored so far in this book, radiocarbon and DNA testing of the skulls has never been performed, added to the ambiguity of who they may have been.

My reasoning for including extensive descriptions of the enigmatic stone work at Tiwanaku/Puma Punku and Sillustani is that you will see there is a somewhat direct correlation between megalithic works in Peru and Bolivia with the presence of elongated skulls, which is quite curious. We will see many more examples of this relationship as the book proceeds. I am not saying that the megalithic works were created by the people whose skulls are found in these locations, since radiocarbon tests have largely not been done, but it could imply that the skulls are of descendants of such builders.

So far we have found that most of the sites where we find examples of ACD do correspond quite well with the "path of Viracocha." This next place deviates somewhat from this pattern geographically, but ties in culturally. A study from the 1990s compares human skeletal samples from Tiwanaku to those from the Moquegua Valley in southern Peru to test the proposed model which posits migration from the Altiplano to Tiwanaku 'colonies' in the fertile, lowland region of Moquegua. (73) The Moquegua region is ideal for studying the bio-archaeological implications of Tiwanaku interaction with the periphery because Tiwanaku's influence in the valley has been clearly established, intensive archaeological investigations and ceramic chronologies allow for tight temporal control, and a large collection of pre-Tiwanaku and Tiwanaku human skeletal remains is available.

The basic conclusions from the examinations of skeletal materials from the Moquegua Valley show a strong correlation with those of Tiwanaku, including time periods based the existence of predominately Tiwanaku style pottery. The study cites 'our research also indicates that while the individuals in Moquegua appear to be members of 'Tiwanaku' in all ways, they displayed differences from other Tiwanaku- affiliated sites in the altiplano in the ways in which they culturally modified their head shapes. The implications of this are not entirely clear.'

Unfortunately the article does not contain photos of what these "differences" were. Prior to the Tiwanaku influx, an earlier culture called the Huaracane lived in the area, but there are no references that could be found as to whether they performed ACD. Thus, it is possible that the people of Moquegua performed variations of ACD as a way to be distinct from their Tiwanaku forebears, or as the result of local influence, but all of this is speculation on the author's part at this point.

12: Colca Canyon

Elongated skulls in a chullpa at Colca Canyon

Now, we deviate back towards the "path of Viracocha" as we look north to the next location where elongated skulls are found; in the Colca canyon region. About 1,400 years ago, the Collagua, who were supposedly Aymara from Tiwanaku, and the Cabana, who were of Quechua origin, both pre-Incan people with an advanced level of agricultural development, carved out 8,000 hectares of terraces on the slopes of the canyon, in order to cultivate and control the irrigation. The terraces are used to this day. (74)

Skulls, including elongated ones near Colca Canyon

The Cabana favoured wide and flat skulls as a tribute to their mythical place of origin, (not listed) and the Collagua, tall and elongated skulls, so that they can be differentiated from the Cabanas. The Spanish found this practice grotesque and went on to ban its practice. (75) What is intriguing about this is that here you see cultural distinctions between the dominant societies of the Andes regions of Peru and Bolivia, as in the Quechua and Aymara, as expressed in skull shape. So far we have seen relationships between Aymara and pre-Aymara people and ACD, but as we travel north from here on, the Quechua influence, from which, for example the Inca arose, is beginning to take effect.

13: Andahuaylillas: Huayqui

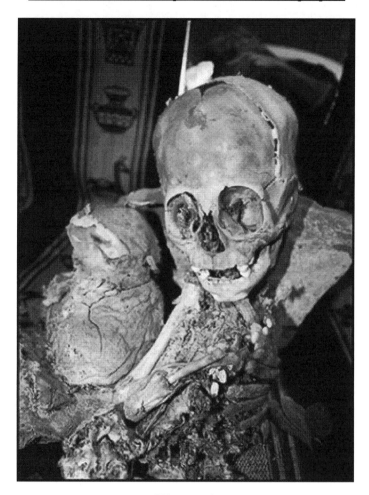

Huayqui

Now we veer back along the "path of Viracocha" to the northwest of Colca Canyon, and the presence of elongated skulls very much intensifies. One hour drive south of Cusco, capital of the Inca there is a small museum run by anthropologist Renato Davila. Sr. Renato's museum contains artifacts that he collected from the area, including Inca pottery, stone implements and some elongated skulls. But his prize find and exhibit id a 50 cm long skeleton which has completely perplexed not only the archaeological community, but also medical experts from various countries who have come to examine "Huayqui" (Inca quechua term meaning "friend" or "equal") in person.

Huayqui was found by Sr. Renato in an ancient grave yard, a few kilometers away from where the museum is located in the small town of Andahuaylillas. While searching for meteorites which are common to the area on the flank of Mount

Viracochan (as in Viracocha) he stumbled across an opened grave which had been plundered by local, one presumes, tomb robbers.

There on the side of the tomb was the Huayqui skeleton, missing both legs, one arm, and both hands. In other words, only the skull, neck and chest/abdomen were more or less intact. What Sr. Renato found, rescued and now proudly displays is perhaps the only skeleton of its kind on public display in Peru.

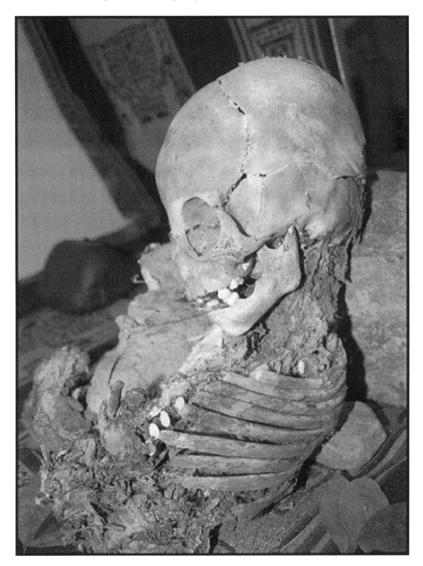

The possibly unique specimen called Huayqui

So what makes this so special? For starters, the skull is the size of the torso, which is not only irregular, but has stunned the more than 20 foreign doctors, nurse, dentists and other medical professionals who have seen it in person with the author. None of the above have been able to explain any medical condition that could have caused the skull to be so huge in comparison with the size of the body.

Some, non-medically trained people believe that the size and shape of the head are the result of hydrocephalus, also known as "water on the brain." The term hydrocephalus is derived from the Greek words "hydro" meaning water and "cephalus" meaning head. As the name implies, it is a condition in which the primary characteristic is excessive accumulation of fluid in the brain. The "water" is actually cerebrospinal fluid (CSF) clear fluid that surrounds the brain and spinal cord. The excessive accumulation of CSF results in an abnormal widening of spaces in the brain called ventricles. This widening creates potentially harmful pressure on the tissues of the brain. (76)

Thanks to the work of Dr. Theo Paredes of Cusco, who is an anthropologist, a film crew from the Science Channel visited Peru in January of 2014 and made a 20 minute documentary about Huayqui. Theo was in charge of the process of assembling a team of medical professionals, anthropologists and archaeologists, as well as the author to do a thorough examination of Huayqui.

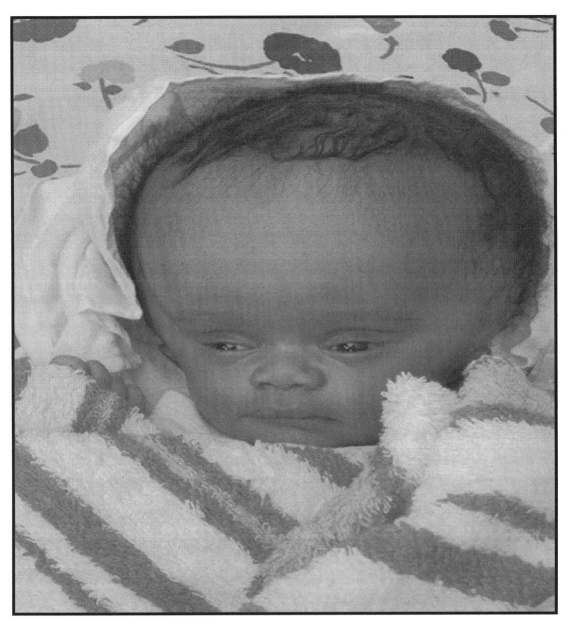

This is what hydrocephaly looks like

A Cusco based radiologist, Dr. Eric Flores after looking at x ray scans of Huyaqui's skull and the skeleton itself remarked that he saw no signs of known disease, nor evidence of ACD; it was his opinion that Huayqui was born with that shape of skull. Also, he was able to discount the idea that Huayqui suffered from hydrocephaly. Another insight by Dr. Flores was that there appeared to be a fracture in the lower left side of the skull, and lack of any bone tissue repair suggested that Huayqui died a violent death.

Another feature of Huayqui's skull that almost everyone notices is the size of the eye sockets, which are much larger than normal, more vertically than horizontally so, and seemingly shallow. Dr. Alcides Vargas, the director of the clinic where Huayqui was examined remarked the eyes had to have actually protruded, quite unlike a normal human. Aw well, the nasal septum is unusually small, meaning that Huayqui most likely had a very flat nose, not a characteristic of someone from the highlands of Peru where it was found. Also, the anterior fontanel, which is where the frontal and left and right parietal bone plates of the skull fuse at about 2 years of age (also known as a baby's "soft spot") is still open in Huayqui, and thus most estimates are that it died at about 20 months of age. However, the Cusco neurologist was able to calculate the brain volume that Huayqui would have had, and believed it to be 50 percent larger than a normal 2 year old child. Dr. Vargas' overall opinion is that he has never seen anything like Huayqui before in his extensive medical career.

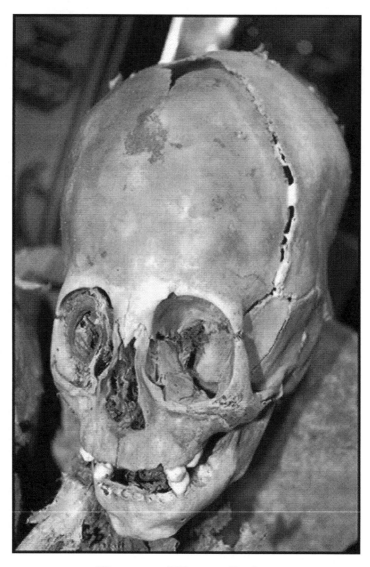

Close up of Huayqui's face

Although a PhD archaeologist in Cusco believed it to be a case of ACD, the shape being the result of stiff boards being placed at the front and back of the head and then wrapped with a textile, a CT three dimensional scan was also performed on Huayqui. ACD would change the shape, but not the volume of the skull cavity, and when neurologist Dr. Carlos Perez examined the CT results, he noted that Huayqui's skull volume is 169 cm, 50 percent larger than that of a normal 2 year olds. He called it a "natural skull with inexplicable proportions" and could find no other skull in the medical literature that resembled Huayqui.

Dr. Theo Paredes, after completing the documentary believes, as does the author that Huayqui could represent an example of a branch of humanity that went extinct. Though most scientists believe that they completely understand the human family tree, new finds appear from time to time that question their confidence, and their actual knowledge.

For example, in 2003, archaeologists working on the remote Indonesian island of Flores found the remains of 9 individuals, including one complete skull which died about 13,000 years ago. The adults were only about 3 feet 6 inches tall, and were determined to be a species different than us, called Homo floresiensis. (77) In order to see if this could be the case with Huayqui, Dr. Paredes arranged for radiocarbon dating, and found out that Huayqui died between 1275 and 1390 AD. Thus, he or she lived when the Inca culture was dominant in the area.

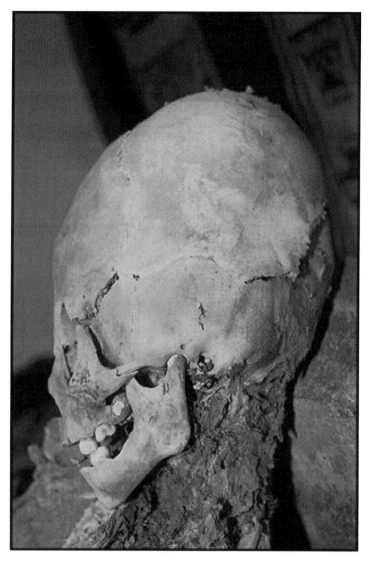

Profile of Huayqui's head

Initial DNA testing was also conducted. Mitochondrial DNA was successfully extracted, and the mother was determined to be human, however, the testing did not assess what the ancestry of the mother was. Far more surprising and confusing was that they could not identify what species the father was. Dr. Paredes theorizes that Huayqui was some kind of hybrid, and not necessarily from this planet.

He decided to consult with Cusco shaman Willco Apaza, who tells him about an Inca oral tradition about a being called Orejones. In the distant past, when there was an eclipse, a lighted hole opened in the sky and out came a very large "man" with an elongated skull and ears and a flattened nose.

Other doctors who have examined Huayqui in person note that the one arm which remains, minus the hand is composed of bones much longer than those of a 2 year old child, and that the number of ribs are different than a normal human. Most people have 24 ribs (78) while Huayqui has 20, and one anatomy expert remarked that its ribcage appears to be upside down. It must be stressed that none of the medical experts interviewed believe that Huayqui is fake, as in being made of plastics or composites, nor an assemblage of the bones of different human or animals.

Another curious aspect as about Huayqui is the teeth. There were originally 10 teeth in its mouth, which is consistent with it being a 2 year old human (79.)

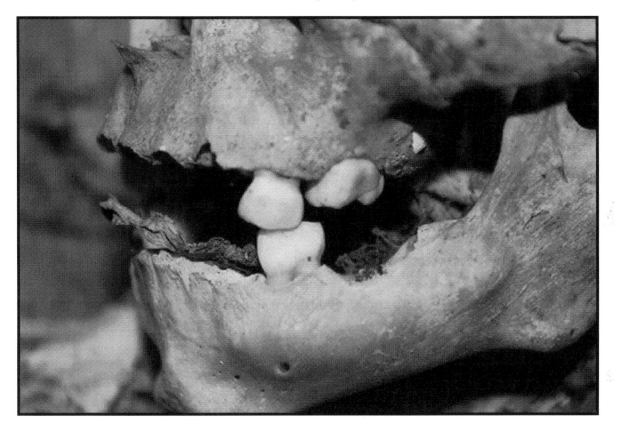

The remarkable teeth of Huayqui

At this age, the teeth are of course what are called deciduous or baby teeth, but what is striking about Huayqui is that the teeth appear to be secondary or those of a developing adult, which has shocked dentists who have visited the museum. As well, when the x rays were conducted thanks to Dr. Theo Paredes, there were no signs whatsoever that other teeth were developing below the ones in Huayqui's mouth.

There are also other anomalies to be found in the immediate area of where Huayqui once lived. At the Huaro museum, located in a small town of the same name 10 minutes' drive south of Andahuaylillas. Aside from Inca pottery, and artifacts from other cultures that once lived in the area, there are stone remnants of ancient presumed plumbing which do not fit in with the at best Bronze Age technology which these people had.

Strange undeciphered inscriptions in Huaro

As well, stacked against the walls are flat stones inscribed with symbols that are unique to the area. Sr. Renato Davila has attempted to translate their meaning in a book he has published, but it is likely that their true original meaning is lost in the mists of time.

Perhaps the most prized artifact in the collection is the full mummified skeleton of a royal woman, presumed to be adolescent in age, whose head features, including face have been reconstructed. She had an elongated skull, and was found in the same ancient cemetery as Huayqui; no wonder this area has been known for centuries, at least, as the "Valley of the Wizards."

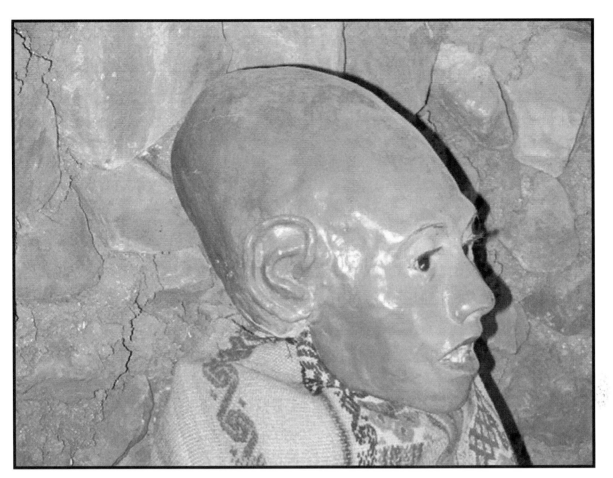

Teenage royalty with elongated head

14: Cusco

We now move northwest, along the "path of Viracocha" and in fact on the ancient Inca road which is the modern highway to Cusco, capital of the Inca culture. What is quite intriguing is that the Inca road and "path of Viracocha" line up almost perfectly from Potosi, through Oruro, Tiwanaku, Island of the Sun, Sillustani, Andahuaylillas, Cusco, Ollantaytambo, Machu Pic'chu, Huanuco, Pataz Province and Cajamarca; all places where we find elongated skulls.

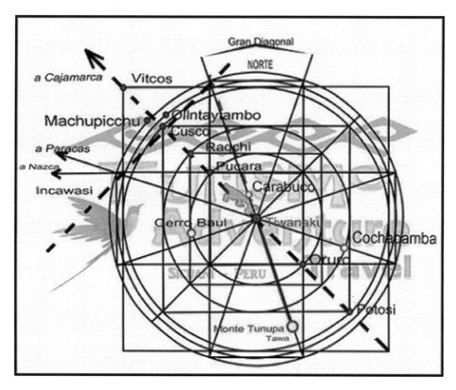

Path of Viracocha

Though the Inca are the most famous pre-Colombian culture of South America, much of their history was wiped out, on purpose by the Spanish conquistadors and their descendants, especially the Catholic Church. So zealous was their contempt and ignorance of all things Inca that most aspects of this great people was ruthlessly destroyed. A major example of this was the collecting and burning of one of the Inca forms of coded information, the Khipu.

The word khipu comes from the Quechua word for "knot" and denotes both singular and plural. Khipu are textile artifacts composed of cords of cotton or occasionally camelid fiber. The cords are arranged such that there is one main cord, called a primary cord, from which many pendant cords hang. There may be additional cords attached to a pendant cord; these are termed subsidiaries. The Inka used a decimal system of counting. Numbers of varying magnitude could be indicated by knot type and the position of the knot on its cord. (80) Though usually numerical in nature, and generally used for accounting purposes, Dr. Gary Urton of Harvard University is working on the concept that some of the Khipu could be a coded language.

Even the origin of the Inca, and when they established Cusco as their capitol are open to speculation as a result of the appalling attempts by the conquistadors and the Catholic Church to basically wipe out Inca history. Most believe that the Inca lived on the Island of the Sun, Island of the Moon and on the nearby Copacabana Peninsula of present day Bolivia prior to migrating north to the Cusco and Sacred Valley area.

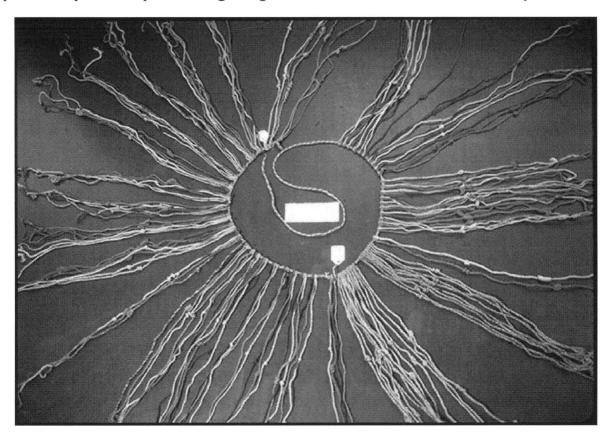

Classic Inca Khipu

Although the history of the Incas prior to their arrival in the Cusco valley is not evident in any archaeological finds, legend tells of the first man and woman, created by Viracocha arising from Lake Titicaca, about 250 miles to the southeast of Cusco, seeming to indicate local origin of the tribe. Another theory, which refutes the idea of indigenous origin, is that of Polynesian decent, formed on the basis of both Indian legend and linguistic similarities. The legend states that on the northern coast of Peru once landed a great chief, already ruler of an advanced civilization, who eventually situated his people inland and had a "long and prosperous reign," about which there is no further information. However, anthropologists who subscribe to this theory state that the landing site alone provides enough information to deduce that the migration of these legendary people must have originated in the west, perhaps Fiji or Easter Island, and not in southern Peru. (81) There are many linguistic similarities between the Maori language of Easter Island and New Zealand with the Inca Quechua, including the word "Inca" which means leader or warrior in both.

The origins of the Inca are murky, but in pre-Inca times, Cusco was located at a nexus point between two earlier empires, one called the Wari and another based at the city of Tiwanaku. This central location gave the Inca a number of advantages when they were able to expand, one of the most important being the availability of infrastructure, which these earlier empires had already created. (82)

Study of the origin and development of the Inca state has been hindered by the fact that comparatively little archaeological investigation of Inca antecedents has been carried out in the Inca heartland, the Valley of Cusco. In recent years, most scholarship has been devoted to developing the broad outlines of Peruvian prehistory in pan-Andean terms. While an overarching view of the cyclical development and decline of complex society in the Andes has provided a general framework for viewing the growth of social complexity, more specific information is needed on local sequences of events. (83)

Pre-Inca megalithic entrance to Cusco

As regards the Inca having elongated skulls, there is scant information, though many skulls of this nature are labelled "Inca" without there being much data in terms of radiocarbon or DNA testing. However, if their origins were in the Lake Titicaca area, their association with the elongated skulls of the ruling class of the Tiwanaku can be inferred, since both the end of the Tiwanaku culture and arrival of the Inca in the Cusco area are by many accounts very close in chronological terms. Also, there is evidence, though oral tradition and not scientific, that elongated skulls also had a presence on Easter Island and other parts of Polynesia in the distant past.

The great Peruvian writer Garcilaso de la Vega, (1539 to 1616) whose mother was of royal Inca birth, describes that ACD was common in Cusco among the royal Inca classes prior to the Spanish arrival; boards were placed on the front and back of the skull soon after birth and a cloth wrapped around the head which was tightened daily until the child was 4 or 5 years old. Decrees were made under Spanish rule, with the first being in 1567 by the Provincial Court in Lima (84) and two others in 1573 and 1575 prohibiting any Natives from performing ACD on children, thus, about this time the elongated skulls of Peru came to an end.

There are no portraits of Inca with elongated skulls that the writer knows of, mainly because the Inca were not makers of portraits of their rulers, and in fact much of their art is of poor quality when compared to other Native cultures of Peru and Bolivia. All depictions of the Inca, who were the royal ruling family and not a term to be used to describe the general population of the area were made soon after the Spanish conquest, or later.

One fact that most people do not realize is that there were few royal Inca in existence when the Spanish arrived in Peru.

Possible look of an Inca ruler

The last true Inca ruler, Huayna Capac died of smallpox in about 1527, 5 years before the arrival of the conquistadors and upon his death rule of the Inca world was divided in two. His son Atahualpa was given the northern area, basically modern day Ecuador to steward, while another son Huascar was given care taking of the rest. After 5 years of relative peace Atahualpa's forces attacked Huascar and most of the royal Inca family in Cusco, resulting in the slaughter of almost all of them.

Depiction of an Inca ruler with symbolic elongated head?

Two of the few that survived included the writer Garcilaso de la Vega's mother and uncle, and thus this more or less brought an end to the pure royal Inca bloodline. What the above tells us is that since there are no portraits of what the pure Inca look like, and that the vast majority were killed off in 1532, we can't be sure that they had elongated heads, whether via ACD or as some genetic trait. There are many photos on the internet which are labelled "Inca skulls" but none to the author's knowledge have been either radiocarbon or DNA tested to prove the authenticity of this labelling. Three museums in the city of Cusco have elongated skulls on display, and all are reported to be Inca, though again radiocarbon and DNA testing have not proven this. The first is the Inca Museum just west of the central Plaza de Armas, which has about half a dozen skulls. Most show obvious signs of ACD but one, seemingly of a toddler of less than 2 years, according to doctors that have seen it with the author, is quite perplexing. The skull is oval in nature, and does not show flattening on the front or back which is what one would expect if still boards and textile were used to alter the head shape.

Another small museum is located underground in front of the Coricancha, which was the sacred center of the Inca from the earliest of days. There are more than 10 skulls on display, with 4 lined up in a row. They are classic "cone head" shapes and two appear to lack the sagittal suture that every living human has.

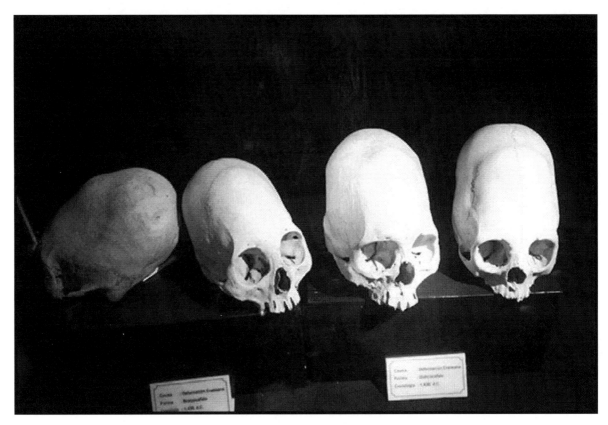

4 "Inca" skulls in the Coricancha Museum

As you will see farther along in the book, this lack of a suture is one of the characteristics which may distinguish between ACD and the possibility that some of the elongated skulls of Peru and Bolivia were born that way.

The third museum is dedicated to artifacts returned from Yale University to Peru; found by American adventurer Hiram Bingham III during excavations at Machu Pic'chu from about 1911 to 1915. Bingham found more than 100 skeletons in various tombs and caves in this Inca citadel, half of them being male and the other half female, and some had elongated skulls.

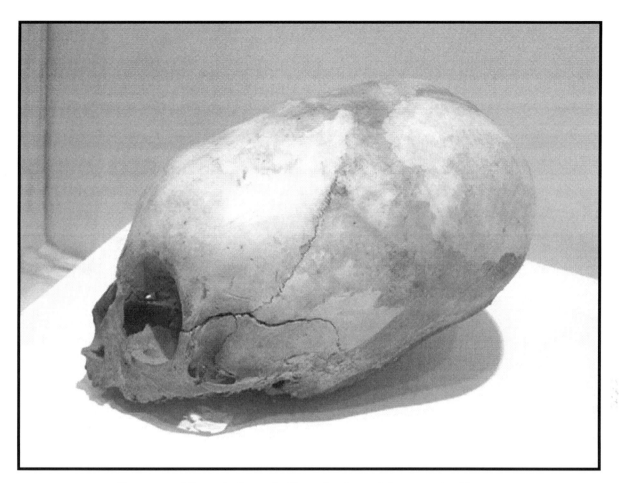

Presumed Inca infant skull at the Inca Museum in Cusco

It is presumed by most academics, but not proven, that the Inca were the first inhabitants and builders of Machu Pic'chu.

Brian Bauer, an expert in Andean civilization at the University of Illinois at Chicago and a National Geographic grantee, says Machu Pic'chu, which he believes was built around 1450 AD was, in fact, relatively small by Inca standards and maintained only about 500 to 750 people. One thing is certain, says Bauer, archaeological evidence makes it clear that the Inca weren't the only people to live at Machu Pic'chu.

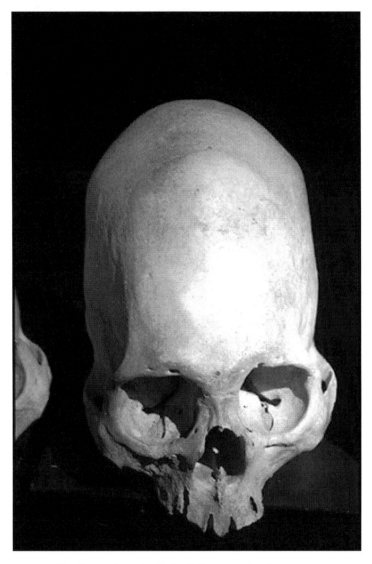

Coricancha skull lacking sagittal suture

The evidence shows, for instance, varying kinds of head modelling, as in ACD, a practice he claims is associated with peoples from coastal regions as well as in some areas of the highlands. Additionally, ceramics crafted by a variety of peoples, even some from as far as Lake Titicaca, have been found at the site. (85) Again, as far as the author knows no radiocarbon or DNA testing has been conducted on the elongated skulls of Machu Pic'chu.

Quotation from Spanish Conquistador
PEDRO PIZARRO (1571) about Peru:

"The ruling class in the kingdom of Peru was fair-skinned with fair hair about the color of ripe wheat. Most of the great lords and ladies looked like white Spaniards. In that country I met an Indian woman with her child, both so fair-skinned that they were hardly distinguishable from fair, white men. Their countrymen called them 'children of the gods'."

Quote supposedly from Pedro Pizarro

An interesting phenomenon that Francisco Pizarro, leader of the Spanish conquistadors is said to have observed was the presence of light skinned people with dark red hair in Cusco. When he enquired as to who they were, the response was "the last of the Viracochas." (86)

15: Ollantaytambo

Megalithic and Inca core of Ollantaytambo

Following the "path of Viracocha" we next reach Ollantaytambo, which one of the largest of the Inca ruins. During the Inca civilization, Ollantaytambo was believed by some to have been the royal estate of the high Inca Pachacutec who conquered the region, built the town and a ceremonial center. At the time of the Spanish conquest of Peru it served as a stronghold for Manco Inca Yupanqui, leader of the Inca resistance. (87) However, Ollantaytambo is such a massive site, and very complex in terms of the various construction methods used, that it may have been built over the course of many generations of Inca.

The museum located in the town of Ollantaytambo has unfortunately been closed for many years, and so the author has never had access to it, but it is rumoured to have elongated skulls in its collection. Local experts have stated that an ancient cemetery containing elongated skulls exists at the base of the mountain facing Ollantaytambo, below what some, including the author think is a carved human profile. The face itself is known, interestingly enough, as Tunupa or Viracocha, who is believed to have visited the area in the distant past as a teacher of arts and sciences.

An expedition was carried out with Los Angeles based researcher and author L.A. Marzulli in January of 2013 to find the grave yard. After climbing through dense bush, over rock piles and consulting with local farmers, we were able to find a few skulls exhibiting ACD, but our informants told us that in the past there were many more, of much greater size and complexity.

However, it is at the quarry where the megalithic blocks which make up some of the most interesting of Ollantaytambo's constructions are that more interesting skulls exist, or perhaps existed. The quarry called Kachiqhata is located 5 kilometers from the site, commonly called the Sun Temple at Ollantaytambo where we find finely hewn rhyolite stones tightly fitting together; some weighing more than 60 tons.

Profile of Viracocha or Tunupa at Ollantaytambo

How the stone was actually cut, shaped and transported from the quarry which is actually the top of a mountain to Ollantaytambo remains a mystery. The idea that teams of Inca workers did this is laughable, since rhyolite is a very hard granitic stone containing a high percentage of quartz crystal, which Inca bronze tools could not hope to cut.

Skull found at the base of the Viracocha profile

In a cave below the main quarry there are the remains of skeletons with elongated skulls, still in the traditional fetal position, which was common in many cultures in Peru and Bolivia. Unfortunately one skeleton which was completely intact, including a very large skull was badly damaged prior to the author's visit to the site, with the skull itself having been removed, and most likely stolen. Such defamation of ancient places is not uncommon in Peru as well as other countries, and fine examples of elongated skulls can be sold, completely illegally on the international black market for more than 1000 US dollars.

Skeletal parts found in the cave

16: Abancay

Following the "path of Viracocha" our next site of interest is Machu Pic'chu, and elongated skull remains found there have already been discussed. So now we have to veer left, and follow an ancient Inca road which connects the "path of Viracocha" (called the Qhapaq Nan, or royal road) with the other major Inca road at the Pacific Ocean.

As we have seen, the "path of Viracocha" follows, and in fact is the Inca Qhapaq Nan moving from the northwest of Peru, at the border with Ecuador down through and past Lake Titicaca. Perhaps simply due to the shape of the coast of Peru, a seaside route, which is the modern Pan-American highway built on top of an Inca (and perhaps older) runs parallel to the Qhapaq Nan. There are numerous roads that connect these two major Inca routes, and the one we will be following connects Cusco with the Pacific at the town of Pisco, which itself is an Inca name meaning "many birds" as the ocean area there is astonishingly productive.

Our first stop is the town of Abancay which was already a populated area before the arrival of the Incas. It was the frontier of the Quechua-Inca cultural influence area of the Chanca, an ethnic native group of Peru, descended from the Wari. Its name comes from a flower native to the region called amankay. (88) Here there is a small regional museum which is called Museo Arqueologico y Antropologico De Abancay Illanya and houses, on display about 10 elongated skulls, all which seem to be examples of ACD except for one, which is that of a very young child. The museum director told us that all were Wari culture skulls, which would more or less date them at being from 700 to 1100 AD (89) however, once again, no DNA or radiocarbon testing has been done, so the dating is based most likely on ceramics or other artifacts found with the skulls.

Display of skulls in Abancay museum

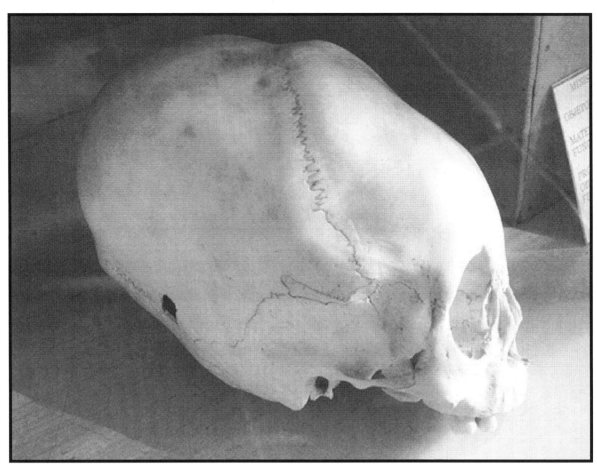

Elongated skull of very young child at Abancay museum

17: Ayacucho

As we follow the Inca road along we next stop in the area of the city of Ayacucho, where two fine museums are to be found having elongated skulls. The first is at the large archaeological site called Wari, (or Huari) obviously named after the pre-Inca culture discussed earlier in this book. In 1550, the chronicler Pedro Cieza de Leon recounted the discovery of several monumental structures approximately 25 km (15 miles) from the city of Huamanga, whose architecture differed from previously discovered Inca structures. He was describing Wari, the capital of the first Pan-Andean state, from the pre-Inca period (between 600 and 1000 A.D.) (90)

Wari is an example of urban planning using pre-Hispanic engineering techniques. The urban core, which spanned some 400 hectares and at its peak was home to some 40,000 inhabitants, was strategically located in a position with rapid access to the coast and the inland jungle, mid-way between the northern and southern mountain ranges, where they established administrative centres and colonies.

As we have seen earlier, the Wari were in many ways influenced by the Tiwanaku culture, so the questions arise; could ACD among the Wari have been as the result of Tiwanaku influence? And did the Inca practice also come from their affiliation with, or even genetic descent from the Tiwanaku?

Interesting shaped stones on the right; two of many

Although the site seems clearly to be from the Wari period, as at other sites like Tiwanaku, Puma Punku, Cusco, Ollantaytambo and others there are stone artifacts which appear to be quite out of place with the bronze age Wari culture. As the photos show, multiple examples of large holes drilled through hard stone can be found which seemingly once fit together as perhaps a drainage system. As well, a massive box made up of well hewn slabs of volcanic stone at nearby Cheqowasi would appear to have been recycled by the Wari from an earlier, more advanced civilization. Once again, the elongated skulls are presumed Wari, but no DNA or radiocarbon testing on them has been done to the author's knowledge.

Finely hewn slabs at Cheqowasi with Wari wall in behind

In the regional museum in Ayacucho there are 9 elongated skulls on display, once again all estimated to be Wari, without DNA or radiocarbon evidence. 4 of them are what one might best describe as "cone heads" although of course there are more scientific terms used, and most show signs of trepanation, or brain surgery.

Ayacucho Regional Museum skulls

Trepanning, also known as trepanation, trephination, trephining or making a burr hole (the verb *trepan* derives via Old French and therefore via Medieval Latin from the Greek noun of relevant meaning *trypanon*, literally "(a) borer, (an) auger") (91) is a surgical intervention in which a hole is drilled or scraped into the human skull, exposing the *dura mater* to treat health problems related to intracranial diseases.

Elongated skull at the Wari Museum

In ancient times, holes were drilled into a person who was behaving in what was considered an abnormal way to let out what they believed were evil spirits. Evidence of trepanation has been found in prehistoric human remains from Neolithic times onward. (92) Cave paintings indicate that people believed the practice would cure epileptic seizures, migraines, and mental disorders.

In ancient Peruvian practices there is considerable evidence that many of the operations were performed for the naturalistic purpose of removing a bone fragment that had been driven below the surface of the skull vault as the result of an injury, many presumably occurred during hand to hand fighting with stone headed war clubs. A considerable number of trepanned skulls showing effects of battle are those of females and adolescents. These depressed fractures could have created intracranial pressure that resulted in illness and behavioural disturbances. (93)

Several examples of trepanation in Peru

Trepanning was common among the Tiwanaku, Inca, Wari and other cultures with elongated skulls, and some theorize that aside from the process being used to cure head wounds, other medical problems or to release "evil spirits" it could also have been required due to complications from ACD. This could have been the case, but one would think that since this ACD procedure was only performed on members of the royal lineages, that the practitioners would have mastered the technique and that relieving pressure would have been one of their first concerns.

What is perhaps the most amazing aspect is the high degree to which this presumed primitive medical technique was successful as regards the patients' recovery. For example, Andrushko and Verano (2008) analyzed 66 skulls obtained from 11 Cusco region burials in Peru, which exhibited 109 trepanations in all. Most of the methods of trephining these skulls included circular cutting and scraping. They discovered the survival rate among the individuals they analyzed to be 83% evidenced by the well-healed bone of most individuals, some of which exhibited *multiple*, well-healed trepanations. The key hypothesis Andrushko and Verano set out to test was that use of trepanation as a medical treatment as opposed to cultural motivations. What they discovered was that great care was taken to promote healing and prevent infection. The perforations were positioned on the cranial vault so as to avoid musculature and vulnerable regions of the skull like the temporal bones and the nuchal planum of the occipital bone. On one of the individuals that didn't survive the trephination, a clump of organic material was found over the perforation which also included the reinsertion of the excised bone in the cranium. Andrushko and Verano noted the lack of evidence for infection in the skulls they examined and hypothesized that this may have been limited through the application of antiseptics like balsam, saponins, cinnamic acid, and tannin. In support of one of their primary hypotheses, Andrushko and Verano found that 44% of the skulls they examined displayed evidence of cranial trauma adjacent to the site of trepanation, supporting the notion that trepanations among these individuals were motivated by medical treatment rather than cultural practices expected of magic or religious reasons. (94)

18: Inca Wasi And Huaytara

We now travel down the Inca road towards the Pacific, and stop at an archaeological site called Inca Wasi, (Inca house) which is located in the Huaytara Province, Huaytara District, about 25 km from Huaytara, which is a small agricultural town. It is situated at a height of 3,804 m (12,480 ft) and is the most important Inca site in the area.

Megalithic shaping near the Inca Wasi site

There are remains here of important Inca dwellings and walls, but also megalithic structures that may well predate the Inca. By now you will have noticed that where Inca constructions are to be found, we also see evidence of work that was far beyond the capabilities of the Inca's bronze tools, as well as elongated skulls. It seems quite apparent the Inca discovered these more ancient sites during their expansion, and thus, perhaps out of awe, made their own constructions in the same area.

Fine mortar free stone work next to much inferior construction

Modern reverence of the ancient ones

In one trapezoidal niche in the older area of the Inca Wasi rests an elongated skull with various offerings of flowers, fruit, cigarettes and alcohol accompanying it. The author was fortunate that the local caretaker was in attendance.

He told us that elongated skulls are common in the area and that local people, out of reverence for the ancient people still bring offerings to this, and perhaps other elongated skulls.

Elongated head mummies at the museum in Huaytara

The regional museum in the town of Huaytara has some amazing things on display. Along with Inca and other cultures pottery, there are a number of elongated skulls, and most astonishingly, 3 complete mummies with rather large crania.

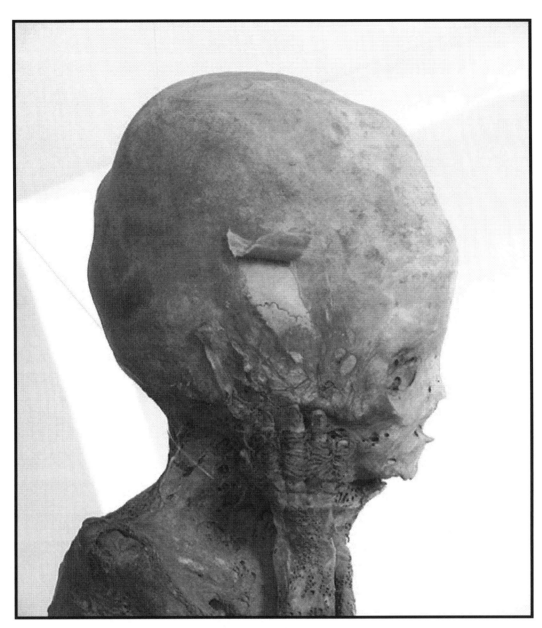

Huge elongated head of presumed child

One would appear to be an adult, and the other two small children. The head of one of the latter is like the Huayqui skeleton of Andahuaylillas, the size of its torso. Upon consulting with the museum director, all were found in the local area, perhaps at Inca Wasi, but he could not shed any light into what culture they were from specifically, and once again no DNA or radiocarbon testing had been done.

Upon asking him if there were any more elongated skulls and perhaps mummies in the museum collection, he stated that they had boxes full of them. Requests to see them were denied, and in fact none of the boxes had been opened for years.

And now we travel closer to the coast of Peru, but before reaching there we make a stop at Tambo Colorado, which actually be called Puka Tambo (red resting place in Quechua.) It was a very important Inca site, said by some to have been made in the 15th century AD by the high Inca Pachacutec, but there is no solid evidence for this claim as regards radiocarbon testing. As the road we have been travelling was most likely the major connector between the Pacific Coast and Cusco, Tambo Colorado was not only a palace for the royal Inca, but also served as a taxation station. Any use of the Inca road system by civilians was subject to a tax of the goods which people would have been carrying to markets, and this process helped in maintenance of said roads. (95)

The onsite museum has no elongated skulls, but more pertinent to this discussion is that although Tambo Colorado is vast and was a major site during Inca times, there is no evidence of megalithic works here, which is curious. We now descend to the Pacific, and perhaps the area which is most important to the discussion of the elongated skulls of Peru and Bolivia; Paracas.

Small wall section of Tambo Colorado

19: Paracas

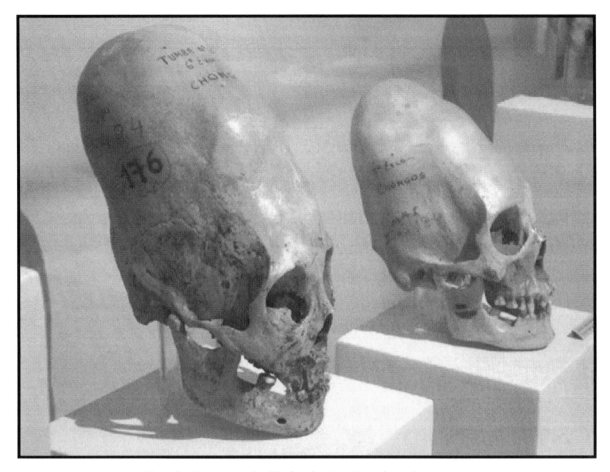

Classic Paracas skulls in the Ica Regional Museum

Archaeologists that the author has spoken with admit that they don't know the origins of the Paracas culture, what language they spoke, or even what they called themselves. The word Paracas comes from the Quechua word *para-ako* (96) meaning "sand falling like rain" and was the name given to the area just south of the city of Pisco by the Inca during their expansion into the area most likely in the 15ᵗʰ century AD. Due to the desert conditions of much of the Paracas area, and high thermal winds which develop during the day, especially in August, it is an apt name. By most accounts, the Paracas culture existed in the region starting from about 800 BC (97) based on preliminary radiocarbon tests of interred organic materials such as textiles, but where they came from before this is unknown.

Very little study of this, one of the most famous of Peru's cultures has been conducted since the pioneering work of Julio C. Tello, (April 11, 1880 – June 3, 1947) who was the "father of Peruvian archaeology" and the first native American to receive a doctorate in that subject. (98)

Tello was born a "mountain Indian" in an Andean village in Huarochiri Province, Peru; his family spoke Quechua, the most widely spoken indigenous language in the nation. He was able to gain a first class education by persuading the Peruvian government to fund it, at first in Peru, and then later on at Harvard in the United States. In 1919 Tello was working with a team at the *Chavin de Huantar* archeological site, where he discovered a stele since named for him, the Tello Obelisk. Construction of the first temple at this major religious center was dated to 850 BC. The work of Tello and others established that the site had been a center of complex culture that lasted for several hundred years, to sometime between 500 and 300 BC.

Tello is best known for his discovery in 1927 of 429 mummy bundles in the *Cerro Colorado* area of Peru on the Paracas Peninsula.

Drawing of Julio C. Tello

He first visited the site on July 26, 1925, following a trail that had begun in 1915 when he had purchased ancient textiles in Pisco. (99) On 25 October 1927, Tello and his team uncovered the first of hundreds of ceremonial mummified bundle burials. He was the first in Peru to practice a scientific method of archeological excavation, to preserve stratigraphy and elements to establish dating and context.

Typical Chavin culture ceramics

It was Tello's belief that the Paracas may have originated in the Chavin area, and he based this on similarities in ceramic styles. However, although Chavin was contemporary with Paracas, the two may have had cultural exchange ties and nothing more.

Paracas ceramic style

The fact that the Chavin culture did not perform ACD is an obvious clue that the Paracas were from a different source, but where? Although Tello took a scientific approach as best he could, radiocarbon testing was not available widely until after his death, and DNA testing has only quite recently reached a level where analysis of ancient human genetics can be relied upon.

Sr. Juan Navarro in his beloved museum in Paracas

As far as the author is concerned, the world authority of the Paracas culture is Sr. Juan Navarro, director of the Paracas History Museum in the town of Chaco, Paracas. Although not an academic with degrees, Sr. Juan was born and grew up in the area, and has been collecting local artifacts for decades. His museum, at which the author is assistant director has more than 45 elongated skulls of the Paracas culture, collected from local individuals who have found them in various locations.

Sr. Juan and guests discussing the Paracas skulls

The Paracas at their peak covered a vast area, from Chincha, about 60 kilometers north of Chaco to the Nazca area, 150 kilometers south, and east into the highlands of Peru. Being largely located at or near the ocean, at least as regards the upper levels of the Paracas society, significant evidence, as shown in Sr. Juan's museum shows that they were masters of the marine environment. They clearly collected all manner of shellfish and other sea foods available at the shore, and netting shows us that they were also able to fish in large quantities.

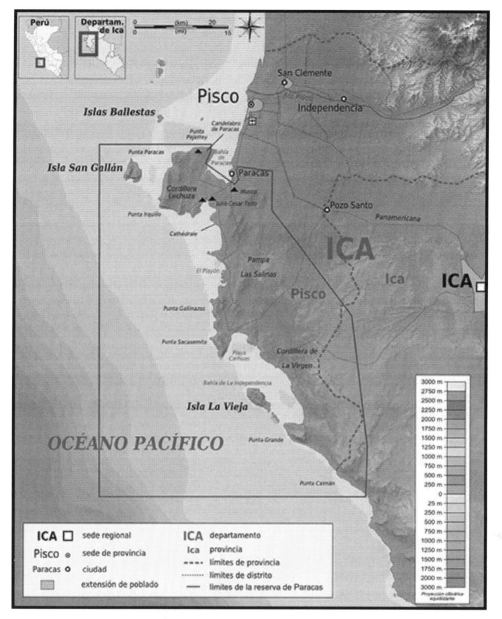

Map of the general Paracas area

As well, the presence of sandals in Sr. Juan's collection indicates that they hunted sea lions, and whale bone implements suggest that they could have been capable of catching these large and fast seagoing creatures as well, unless they harvested stranded ones. Even to this day, sea lions are found in abundance on local islands, and various species of whales and dolphins travel in pods in offshore areas. The question naturally arises as to the nature of the boats or ships that the Paracas could have had to undertake such fishing expeditions. Totora reed is indigenous to the area and is very versatile, still being used, mainly in northern coastal Peru to make houses and shelters, as well as small boats called *caballitos de totora*(little reed horses). (100)

A reed boat is not limited as to how large you can make it. Thor Heyerdahl, the renowned Norwegian explorer most famous for his *Kon Tiki* (name based on Viracocha, who we have discussed) expedition of 1947 where he and his crew successfully sailed from the coast of Peru to Polynesia on a balsa sailing raft also built totora reed boats. (101)

These were named Ra, Ra II and Tigris, and all three were more than 15 meters long and successfully sailed several thousand kilometers each on the open ocean and under full sail. Reed boats, whether they be made from totora, such as on the coast of Peru and in Lake Titicaca or papyrus in the Middle East have been in use for thousands of years. The main body, or hull, usually consists of two large bundles of many long cigar-shaped rolls of reed that can measure 15 meters long or more. Placed between these large bundles is the heart bundle, consisting of three reed rolls stacked together. To join these bundles, a rope is wrapped around the left bundle and the heart bundle while another rope is alternately wrapped around the right bundle and the heart bundle. (102)

Totora boats are still made at Lake Titicaca in Bolivia

The bundles can be made as large as the boat builder's imagination, and it is known that people of the Chincha area, just north of Paracas were great traders in coca, copper and mulla shells using boats going up and down the coast as far as Chile and

Ecuador, returning with other precious items such as emeralds and spondylus shell. (103) These people lived after the fall of the Paracas culture, but before the Inca incursion into the area in the 15th century AD. The ocean current in this coastal area of Peru is called the Humboldt, and also known as the Peru Current. It is an eastern boundary current flowing in the direction of the equator, and can extend 1,000 kilometers offshore. (104)

Spondylus shell in its natural full form

The Chincha or pre-Chincha people took advantage of this current, as well as the prevailing winds which come from the south most of the time, but can also strong from the north on occasion.

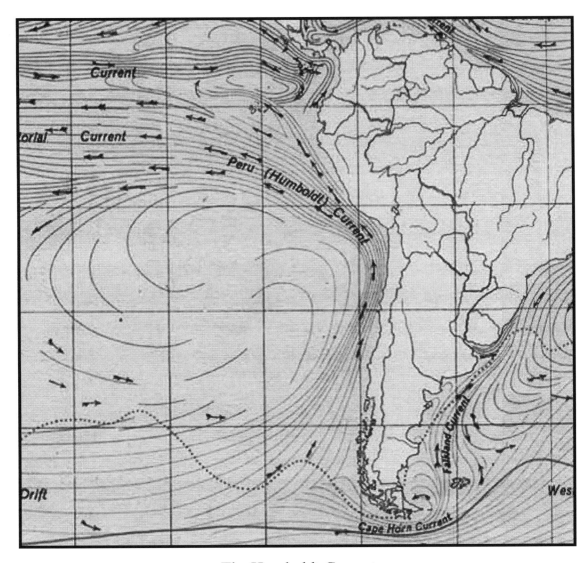

The Humboldt Current

This combination of wind and current allowed them access to Ecuador, and as the current at the equator then moves westward, access to Polynesia and beyond could have been possible, though no artifacts from these areas have been found in Ecuador to the writer's knowledge.

Since the Paracas may well have been sea lion and whale hunters it is conceivable that they too were able to travel vast distances like the Chincha. Evidence for trade with Ecuador can be found in Sr. Juan's museum in Paracas in the form of emerald beads as well as spondylus shells which could only have come from Ecuador, as these materials are not native to Peru. Also, due to the presence of other artifacts which were found with the above items and have been positively identified as Paracas, they must be from that culture. And the likelihood that such items travelled via a land route seems slim to none.

Naturally pigmented and organically cultivated cotton has been produced in Andean South America since at least 2,500 BC. Today, it is grown as a dooryard crop by many peasant and indigenous Indian farmers on the coast and high jungle regions of Peru. Four different cotton varieties are cultivated in three different natural colours (white, brown and green) ranging from beige to light and chocolate brown. (105) Cotton is of course an excellent natural material for making sail cloth, as it is relatively light, strong and dries fast when wet. As the Paracas were master weavers in many ways with cotton and camelid (llama and alpaca) materials, they could quite easily have made sail cloth material. In fact, some Paracas textiles are among the finest ever created not just in Peru, but the planet. As both cotton and totora are natural materials, they are subject to degradation quite rapidly.

Another factor to take into consideration is the huge geoglyph carved into the hard salt encrusted sand hills near the mouth of Paracas bay, which is the largest natural bay on the coast of Peru called the *Candelabra,* or *Candlestick of the Andes.* It measures 181 meters in height (595 feet) and faces north so that it can be seen from a great distance out to sea.

The Candelabra of Paracas

The fact that it is carved into the hard sand 61 centimeters deep also makes it stand out from the landscape. Carbon dating of artifacts found near the glyph date the candelabra to around 200 BC. What it symbolizes is not known for certain; local guides suggest it could be a depiction of a cactus or the Southern Cross constellation; others postulate it to be a landmark made by early sailors representing the lightning rod of the Andean creator god Viracocha. (106) The radiocarbon dating would clearly suggest that the Paracas culture made it, and the Southern Cross has been used for thousands of years as a celestial navigation instrument in the Pacific, especially by the Polynesians.

The Southern Cross on the center right of the photo

Sr. Juan Navarro is in agreement with the idea that the *Candelabra* represents the Southern Cross and in fact is the mirror image of it, with the constellation rising up right behind the geoglyph.

On land, the Paracas were expert agriculturists, growing beans, corn (maize) red peppers, yucca and peanuts, as well as cotton and other plants. (107) In general, the area from Chincha and south through Paracas to the city of Ica is flat, while beyond this, as you approach Nazca it is far more mountainous. Water from the eastern highlands, where there is far more precipitation than the coastal desert natural flows to the ocean both in streams and rivers as well as underground. Also, the climate of this area is very mild, averaging temperatures between 20 and 25 Centigrade year round, and almost constant sunshine. As a result of this agricultural productivity is very high and has been for more than 2000 years; in fact, the climate prior to 2000 years ago was wetter, and thus plant growth may have even been higher.

The water table is very close to the surface due to the flatness of the land in the Paracas area, and therefore the Paracas people did not have to do much irrigating. Also, many of their fields were in fact sunken into the ground by as much as 2 meters, in order for the plants to access the water table more easily.

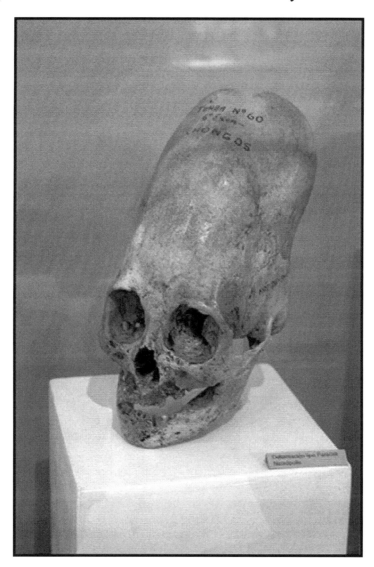

Classic Paracas elongated skull from the Chongos cemetery

As with the other cultures that performed ACD that have been discussed, the Paracas seem to have restricted this practice to only the royal and priestly classes of their quite sizable populations. Their impressive fishing and farming capabilities, which would have been the occupations of a high percentage of the citizens, could have afforded the Paracas elite the resources and time to develop an advanced ceremonial structure, which they in fact had. The amazing ceremonial mantles that they created are among the finest weaving ever made in Peru, and these are only found in royal burial areas, along with elongated skulls.

The grave yards of commoners are quite distinct from those of the Paracas elite. The entire town of Chaco is in fact a vast cemetery, and it is very common for locals to accidentally or on purpose unearth ancient human remains and artifacts of the Paracas, Nazca, Wari, Chincha and Inca people who once lived in the area.

Usually the burials are of fishermen, agricultural workers or other working class people, as evidenced by the simple ceramics and other personal items buried with them. The royal Paracas tombs are basically located in major sites; Cerro Colorado, Cabeza Larga, Chongos and Camacho in the Paracas area, and then Cahuachi, which is a massive ceremonial center near the city of Nazca, in the south. It is at these places that the vast majority of the Paracas culture elongated skulls have been found, and unfortunately have been plundered for many decades by tomb robbers. It is such atrocious and illegal activity that often tip off archaeologists to the locations of ancient cemeteries.

What is quite intriguing is that the shapes of the elongated skulls seem in some ways to be particular to each of at least 4 graveyards. Those from the Cerro Colorado/Cabeza Larga tombs, which are adjacent to one another appear to be swept back in appearance, somewhat like depictions of Akhenaten and the other members of the 18th dynasty period in Egypt.

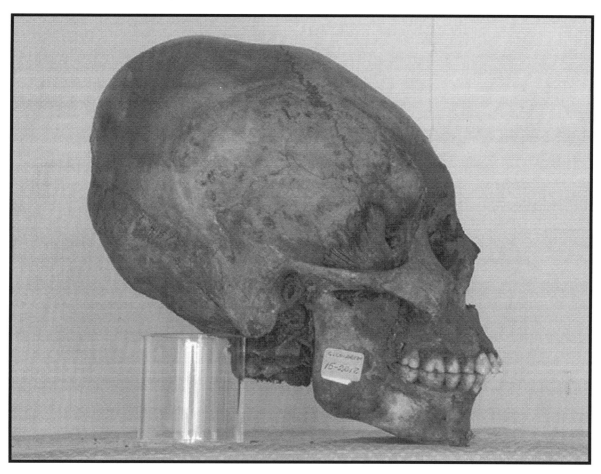

Royal skull from Cerro Colorado

The Camacho ones show the most obvious characteristics of ACD, in that the backs of the skulls are usually very flat; evidence that something rigid like a board or hard cloth was used to shape the head. But perhaps the most intriguing, and perhaps most controversial are those that have been found at Chongos, ones that are very "cone headed" in appearance. All of the cemeteries mentioned above as regards royal burials have beautiful views of the ocean; even Chongos which is many kilometers inland. One can deduce that this was done on purpose to afford those visiting the dead, and perhaps the deceased themselves a breathtaking vista.

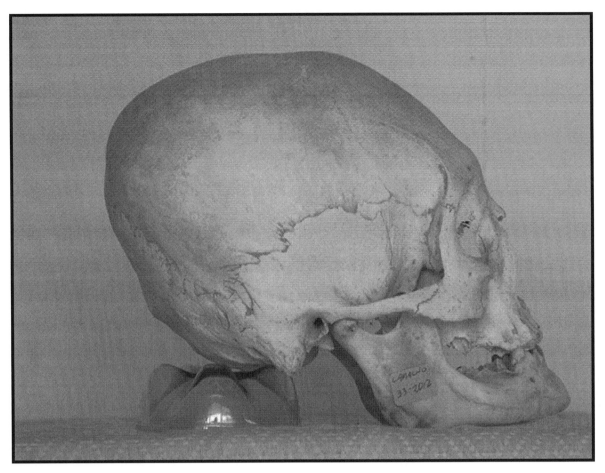

Typical royal skull from Camacho

Chongos is extreme desert bordering very productive farmland and has the remains of adobe pyramidal structures in a sad state of disrepair. According to Sr. Juan Navarro, these temples were created by the Wari culture, but the author thinks otherwise; many similar constructions to the north, in the area of Chincha are believed to have been made at least initially by the Paracas, so why not these as well?

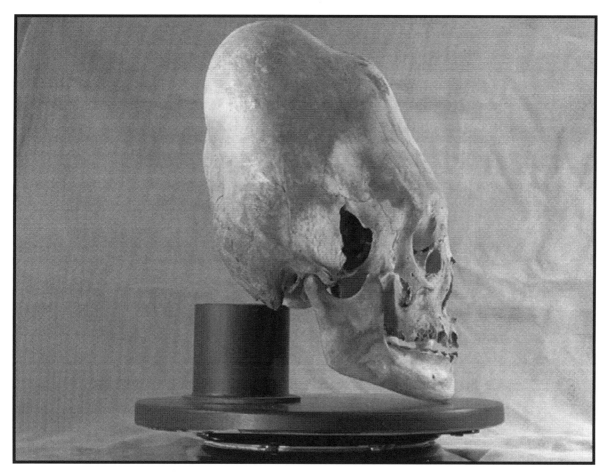

The classic look of the Chongos Paracas

Very close to the largest of these adobe works lie the shattered remains of skulls and other bones of the elongated skull Paracas people whose tombs have been desecrated by tomb robbers for as much as a hundred years. In fact, it is quite possible that the largest and most natural appearing elongated skulls in the world have been found at this location.

Chongos skulls in the Ica Regional Museum

Perhaps the finest example of Chongos skulls on public display are in the Ica Regional Museum in Ica Peru. One in particular has been viewed, at least digitally around the world, and has been mislabeled as being Nephilim, Anunnaki, alien or alien/human hybrid. As it has never been radiocarbon or DNA tested, such claims are based on ignorance and sensationalism. For those that don't know, the Nephilim were a race that came to dominate the antediluvian (pre-flood) world, and are referred to in the Bible as *the heroes of old, men of renown*. They were reportedly the children born to the "*Sons of God*" by the "*daughters of men*", and are described as giants. It is also most important to note that they are mentioned almost simultaneous to God's statement that He would destroy the earth by flood, and it seems from this association that their effect upon mankind was one of the primary justifications that brought the destruction. (108)

According to ancient Mesopotamian mythology, Anunnaki is a word which means: "Princely Offspring" and 'Those of Royal blood' and not the false 'from Heaven to Earth' as some people thought. Anu is the supreme deity in the Sumerian belief system. Ki is the goddess of the Earth. (109) As both the Nephilim and Anunnaki are subjects pertaining to the Middle East, no rational evidence has been presented to the author that they ever existed as well in Peru.

However, there are characteristics of some of the Paracas elongated skulls, especially from Chongos that perplex medical professionals that have visited the Paracas History Museum. They are the following:

1/ Very complex curvature to all aspects of the skull, with no sign of cranially flattening induced by binding materials.

2/ Overly large eye sockets.

3/ No sagittal suture evident what so ever.

4/ Two small holes in the back of the skull.

5/ Very robust lower jaw.

6/ Possible evidence of inherited dental problems.

These will now be discussed one at a time.

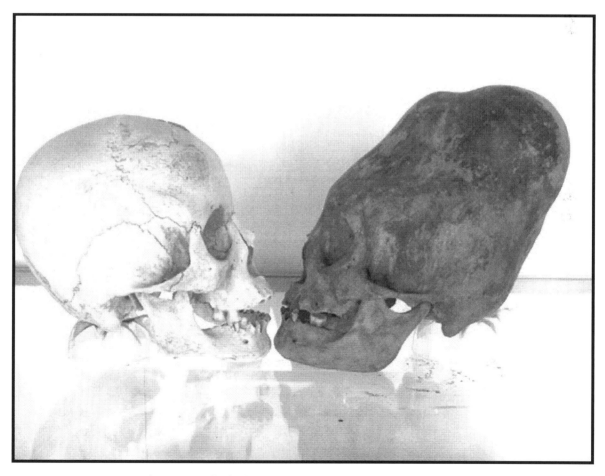

Normal Inca period skull compared with one from Chongos

1/ In a small percentage of the skulls the shape is so complex that simple binding technology does not sufficiently explain how the form was achieved. These are possible candidates for the somewhat controversial idea that some of the Paracas were in fact born with elongated heads, and that their appearance is what caused future generations to have their heads bound in order to match the shape of these progenitors.

What is being proposed is that a somewhat small population of people with elongated skulls once existed, and perhaps migrated to the Paracas area because of its abundant seafood and agricultural possibilities. As few if any other people inhabited the area at their time of arrival, perhaps around 800 BC they could live isolated and in peace. As the population began to possibly dwindle for any of a number of reasons, or simply to develop cultural ties, breeding with residents having normal features could have occurred. Over the course of time the genetic characteristics unique to the Paracas, such as elongated heads would begin to recede, causing the process of ACD to occur in order to maintain their special appearance.

2/ The size of the eye sockets, similar to what the Huayqui skull has not been explainable by the numerous doctors and other medical professionals who have visited Sr. Juan's museum, or the many other examples of Paracas skulls found on the internet. There are at least hundreds of Paracas skulls in museum collections in Peru, and possibly far more located in other countries, as it has been relatively recent for the export of pre-Colombian remains from Peru to be illegal.

3/ The complete lack of a sagittal suture also confounds medical professionals. Sagittal Synostosis is the most common type of premature suture fusion approximately 1 in every 5000 births with a 3:1 male: female ratio. Sagittal synostosis is the premature closure of the sagittal suture, and the child's head shape will be typically narrow from side to side and lengthened from front to back. (110)

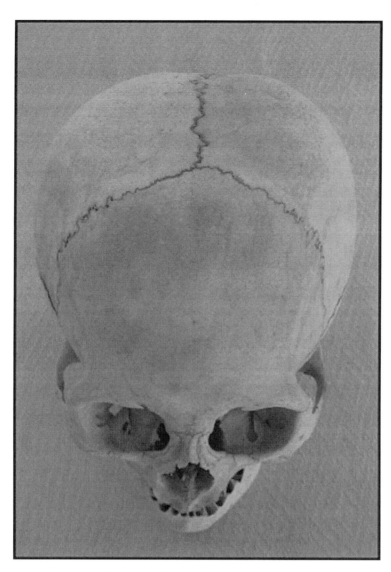

Conventional suture pattern

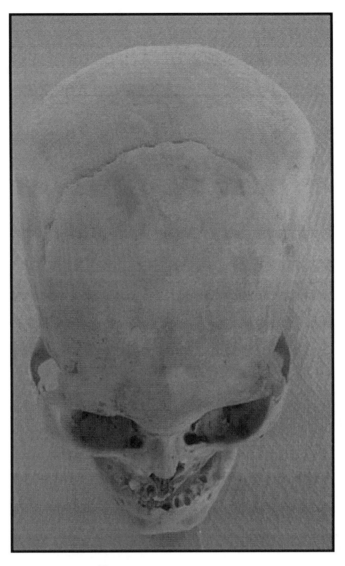

Paracas suture pattern

The sagittal suture does fuse as one ages, usually beginning after someone is about 20 years old and can completely fuse in elderly individuals. (111) However, the ossification that occurs can be clearly seen, as it is in essence the addition of scar tissue. Since premature closure of the sagittal suture causes the skull to grow horizontally, and ossification with age can be seen on the skull, neither can explain why the "cone heads" of some of the Paracas, especially those from Chongos appear to have no sagittal suture what so ever.

4/ The human skull normally has 3 pairs of small holes in the front called the foramen; the zygomaticofacial foramen below and to the outside of the eye sockets, the supraorbital just below the eye sockets and the mental foramen in the mandible or lower jaw. Almost all, if not all of the elongated skulls of the Paracas area also have a fourth pair, called the parietal foramen, which is very uncommon in most human skulls. According to a medical definition: An inconstant foramen in the parietal bone occasionally found bilaterally near the sagittal margin posteriorly; when present, it transmits an emissary vein to the superior sagittal sinus. (112) The superior sagittal sinus is a large vein found in the human head. This vein travels over the top portion of the skull, beginning at the top of the skull and moving to the back part of the skull. At this point, the vein splits into two sections and works to carry blood back to the heart from the vein. (113)

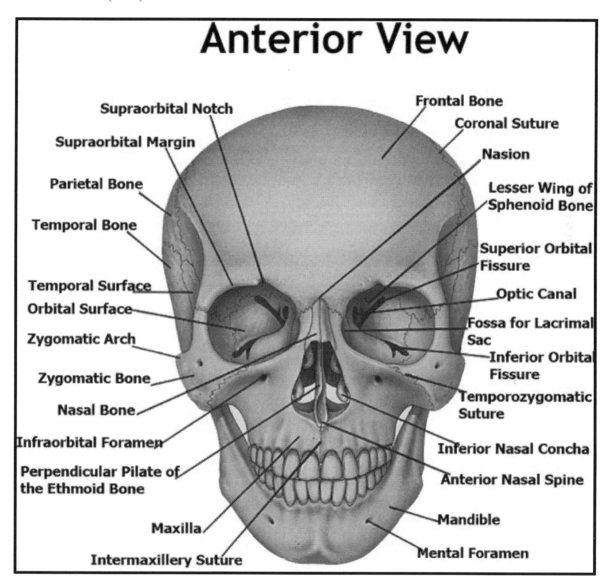

Medical diagram of a human skull

The inference here is that the parietal foramen are present in the elongated skulls to assist in blood flow due to the non-normal shape of the head, and would be an evolutionary development.

5/ The robust jaws common to the Paracas elongated skulls, and much larger than a normal skull may be interpreted as adaptations for masticating a mechanically resistant diet that demanded the generation of a powerful bite force over a broad grinding area of teeth. (114) Such characteristics are more common in early hominins such as Australopithecus rather than modern humans, and would suggest more of a vegetarian than meat based diet.

Parietal foramen in elongated skulls, especially in Paracas

6/ Missing teeth, especially one or more molars is reasonably common in the Paracas elongated skulls, especially those from Chongos, and by missing meaning they failed to ever develop. The term for this is hypodontia, and the cause of isolated missing teeth remains unclear, but the condition is believed to be associated with genetic or environmental factors during dental development.

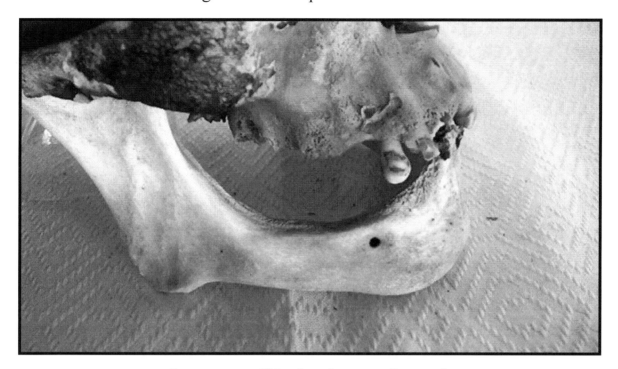

Paracas mandible showing very few teeth

Another interesting feature of Paracas elongated skulls, and elongated skulls in general is the extreme size of the mastoid process, which is a bone projection just behind the mandible. One important role for this bone is as a point of attachment for several muscles: the splenius capitis, longissimus capitis, digastric posterior belly, and sternocleidomastoid. These muscles are one reason the mastoid process tends to be larger in men, because men have bigger muscles as a general rule and thus require larger points of attachment. It is possible that if the Paracas and perhaps other elongated heads were originally natural and thus genetic in nature, that the mastoid process would have to be large to accommodate massive muscles to keep the head upright.

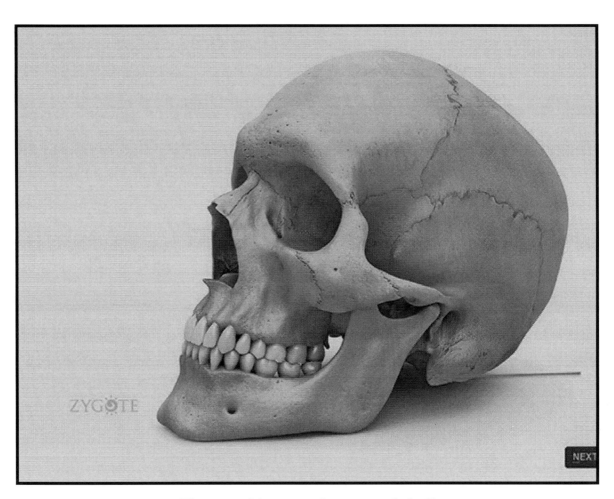

The mastoid process in a normal skull

NEXT

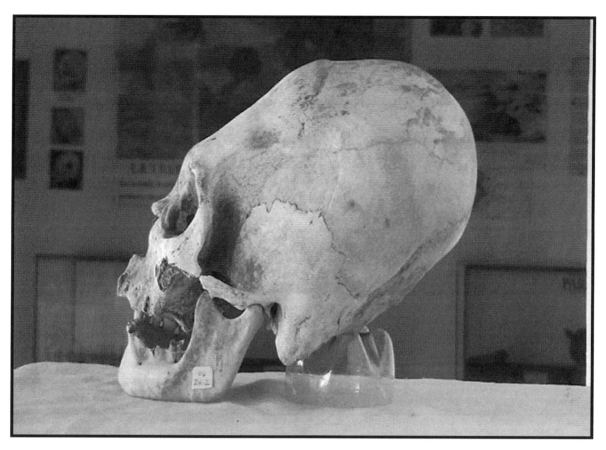

Mastoid process in a Paracas skull

The site of Camacho is also very interesting, for there, like at the other sites mentioned above you can find tombs not only of the Paracas, but also of the Nazca, Wari, Chincha and Inca people. In general, these graves of the different cultures are not mixed together, but are in their own areas, though in many cases heavily congested. In the case of Camacho there is a hill just east of the main cemetery which was recently unearthed by tomb robbers. What it contains are the shattered remains of at least 30 to 50 people who had elongated skulls, and the pottery found with them identify that they were Paracas.

A forensic archaeologist has not yet been to the site to the author's knowledge, and very few people have seen it, but it appears to be a place of absolute carnage. There are no intact skeletons here, it is simply a dense pile of bones of different individuals stacked and strewn in a shallow grave about 15 meters in diameter. All of the skulls found, as has been noted have elongated skulls, but not the "cone head" style found at Chongos.

The possible "killing field" mass grave of Camacho

The Camacho elongated skulls, at least those in this mass grave have flat backs and sloping foreheads, which is the shape that one would expect if ACD was employed. Radiocarbon testing has not been performed on these skulls, but Sr. Juan Navarro believes it to be one of the last of the Paracas grave sites. The Paracas elite with elongated skulls were normally buried with great care due to their social position, and not strewn about in a sordid pile such as witnessed at Camacho. Also, this mass grave is located not in the main Camacho cemetery, but on a nearby hill.

Often the Paracas royalty were buried in vertical family tombs, one carefully stacked on top of or beside another. Or they were buried individually, but always deep, the funeral bundle consisting of multiple layers of finely woven and embroidered fabric which was then covered with layers of sand and small personal items in smaller bundles. (115) The above Camacho cemetery may indicate the scene of a mass killing near the end of the Paracas culture, and now we will explore what may have happened to this very interesting and enigmatic culture.

It has long been recognized that the Nazca culture (ca. 1 to 750 AD) of the Peruvian south coast finds its roots in the Paracas society (800 BC to 1 AD.) Yet the social mechanisms responsible for the innovations that characterize the transition are poorly known. (116) Many academics believe that, in essence, Nazca is merely a continuation of Paracas Culture including the same religious tradition, weaving technology, and general way of life. The decision by archaeologists to recognize a new culture which we call "Nazca" was based on rather arbitrary criteria some think. (117) There are those scholars perceive the Nazca as arising out of the Paracas culture, rather than an in-migration of people from another place. The early Nazca culture arose as a loosely affiliated group of rural villages with self-sufficient subsistence based on corn agriculture. (118) But what these beliefs can't reconcile is at least one major cultural trait; the Nazca do not appear to have been involved in ACD.

Nazca pottery with severed head motif

If the pre-Nazca people who presumably moved into the Paracas territory led to a smooth amalgamation of these two cultures then one would presume that such an important process for the elite, as in ACD would continue as a way to distinguish the ruling classes from the commoners. However, this does appear to be the case. After several years of exploring museum and private collections in the Paracas/Nazca area, little evidence exists of actual Nazca period elongated skulls, most being labelled as pre-Nazca or proto-Nazca, which in essence means the Paracas. It could very well be that the introduction of new groups into the Paracas area was not a pleasant experience for the latter, but was in fact an invasion that terminated the ruling classes of the Paracas elongated skull people.

The Topara culture is thought to have "invaded" from the north at approximately 150 BC. The two cultures then coexisted for one or more generations, both on the Paracas Peninsula and in the nearby Ica Valley, and their interaction played a key role in the development of the Nazca culture and ceramic and textile traditions. (119) Very little is known of the Topara, except that they lived just north of the Paracas territory which stretched just north of the fertile area of Ica. As has been previously written about in this book, the Paracas were masters of agriculture, and the area where the Topara lived was much less productive land. Recent evidence suggests that the Topara were forced out of their area due to local climate change events and thus they moved into the larger and more fertile lands of the Paracas.

The area of coastal Peru is not stable climatically due to the occurrence of El Nino and El Nina events. El Nino and La Nina events are a natural part of the global climate system. They occur when the Pacific Ocean and the atmosphere above it change from their neutral ('normal') state for several seasons. El Nino events are associated with a warming of the central and eastern tropical Pacific, while La Nina events are the reverse, with a sustained cooling of these same areas.

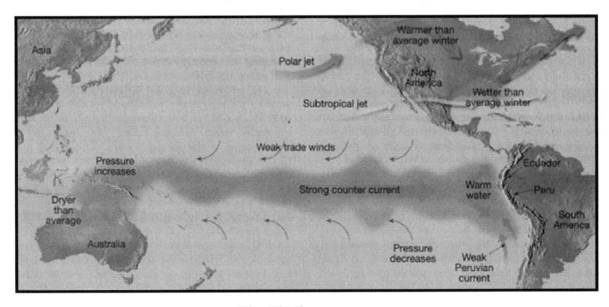

The El Nino process

These changes in the Pacific Ocean and its overlying atmosphere occur in a cycle known as the El Nino Southern Oscillation (ENSO). The atmosphere and ocean interact, reinforcing each other and creating a 'feedback loop' which amplifies small changes in the state of the ocean into an ENSO event. When it is clear that the ocean and atmosphere are fully coupled an ENSO event is considered established. (120)

These two events can cause subtle, or sometimes massive changes in the climate of the Peruvian coast.

For example, around 500 AD, archaeological evidence indicates that the then flourishing Nazca society came to a sudden and bloody demise. Ice core records suggested that severe storms a mega El Nino hit the Peruvian Andes around the time the Nazca's fall began, but this had not been corroborated in the coastal valleys where the Nazca once lived.

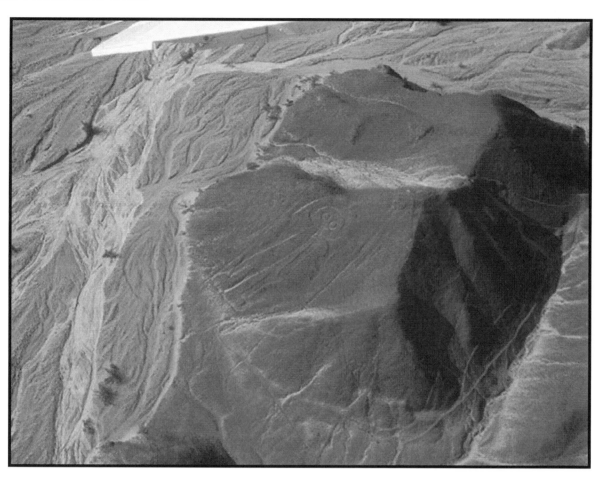

Nazca "astronaut" and signs of flooding

Dr. David Beresford-Jones and his colleagues of the McDonald Institute for Archaeological Research at the University of Cambridge, focusing on the lower Ica valley, solidified this evidence when they discovered a flood layer that sat directly on top of a Nazca rubbish dump. The authors then recreated the flood using a computer simulation, demonstrating that a flood that left such a layer could have caused the damages to the Nazca canal system known to have occurred around 500 AD. (121) It is commonly believed that the famous Nazca lines and geoglyphs were solely created by the Nazca culture, but this is not the case. As has been established earlier, the Candelabra of Paracas has been shown to have been made by the Paracas culture prior to the existence of the Nazca. And, there are many geoglyphs on the way to the

Nazca area that were also created by the Paracas in an area called Palpa. The reason the geoglyphs of Palpa received less attention than those of Nazca may be because the geography of Palpa and Nazca are significantly different. The Palpa region is strewn with continuous abrupt peaks, quite different from the Pampa of Nazca where sands and stone stretch out endlessly over a plain which affords a great deal of visibility. Figures drawn on the mountain side in the Palpa region are less visible, and even disappear depending upon the direction from which they are viewed. (122) Petroglyphs thought to be drawn during the old Paracas Period were discovered in Chichictara, north of Palpa. They are adorable drawings of human beings and animals that look like graffiti drawn by little children. These figures may have depicted the animals that were around them, such as llamas, and people occupying higher stations in the society or high-born and noble people. Many of the figures of people have Tumi, ceremonial knives, in one hand and, in the other hand they hold long bars, possibly a scale indicating a level of rank.

Some of the Palpa geoglyphs as seen from the highway

There are large decorations or something like a hat on the heads. Many of the figures among the Palpa Geoglyphs are similar to these petroglyphs or have human or god-like features related to these petroglyphs. We can see a transition in creative ability in a great number of the figures of human beings that is suggestive of different time periods.

Photo showing the flatness of the Nazca Plain

According to Reindel et al., it was around 1800 to 800 BC when people moved into Palpa. This region had plenty of water at that time and was able to be used as meadow land. It entered a dry period during the Paracas Period (800 to 200 BC.). As it entered the early Nazca Period, the population increased and trading relations with the highland and coastal areas of the Andes were established; however, the weather was becoming more serious. Desertification worsened while unexpected flooding devastated the region a number of times. (123)

The Paracas geoglyph known as the "astronaut"

It seems clear that most of the Palpa figures were created by the Paracas, and many archaeologists also think that the famous "space man" was as well, as the technique used to shape it, and its overall design is different than the other famous Nazca geoglyphs.

What this tells us is that the Paracas were occupying the Nazca area before the Nazca themselves, including the enormous ceremonial city of Cahuachi. Cahuachi, the largest ruins in Nazca, is known as an immense ceremonial center, and a long-term excavation was conducted by an Italian team lead by

Orefici. Ruins with the exact same structure as Cahuachi were uncovered at the Los Molinos excavation in Palpa by the Nasca-Palpa Project. Both sites are located near rivers and on higher ground. Cahuachi is along the Rio Nazca and Los Molinos is located on a section of the Rio Grande just before it branches off into the Rio Palpa. The land stretches out in the direction of the rivers and has a panoramic view of the area.

Reindel believes that Los Molinos was in use between 500 BC and 250 AD. The time that construction began must be traced back even further. According to Orefici, Cahuachi was built between 150 BC and 200 AD. (124) Thus, both at least began as

Paracas sites. Scholars once thought the site was the capital of the Nazca state but have determined that the permanent population was quite small. They believe that it was a pilgrimage center, whose population increased greatly in relation to major ceremonial events. New research has suggested that 40 of the mounds were natural hills modified to appear as artificial constructions. Support for the pilgrimage theory comes from archaeological evidence of sparse population at Cahuachi, the spatial patterning of the site, and ethnographic evidence from the Virgin of Yauca pilgrimage in the nearby Ica Valley. (125)

Reconstructed Sun Temple of Cahuachi

Excavations at Cahuachi have given archaeologists key insights into the culture. The material remains found at the site included large amounts of polychrome pottery, plain and fancy textiles, trace amounts of gold and spondylus shell, and an array of ritual paraphernalia. The remains of pottery found at Cahuachi led archaeologists to believe that the site was specifically non-urban and ceremonial in nature. The debate over the purpose of trophy heads, including those found at Cahuachi continues to this day, whether they were trophies of war or objects of ritual.

Trophy heads of the Nazca; notice the elongated one

Visual depictions of decapitations often associate the decapitators with weapons and military like dress, but such garments could have been worn in purely ceremonial circumstances as well. The term 'trophy head' was coined by the archaeologist Max Uhle, who considered the depiction of severed heads in ancient Peruvian art to correspond to trophies of warfare. Researchers noted that all the heads had one modification in common a hole in the forehead through which a rope could be affixed, presumably so that the severed head can be displayed or carried. (126) Many of the trophy skulls at Cahuachi are elongated, and if we presume them to be Paracas, then it is quite possible that they were either the victims of the Nazca, or were dug up by the Nazca for ritual purposes.

Recent discoveries, as in August of 2014 of more geoglyphs in the Ica/Nazca area which include a snakelike figure roughly 200 feet long, a huge zigzag line, and a giant bird as the result of a massive sandstorm which the locals call a "Paracas" event sheds new light on the area. Pilot and researcher Eduardo Herran Gomez de la Torre, who made the discovery in late July, told the Peruvian newspaper El Comercio that the designs might have been created by the Paracas. While scholars contacted by El Comercio said they suspected the geoglyphs were created during the transition period between the Paracas and Nazca cultures, archaeologists still need to confirm the origin of the designs. (127)

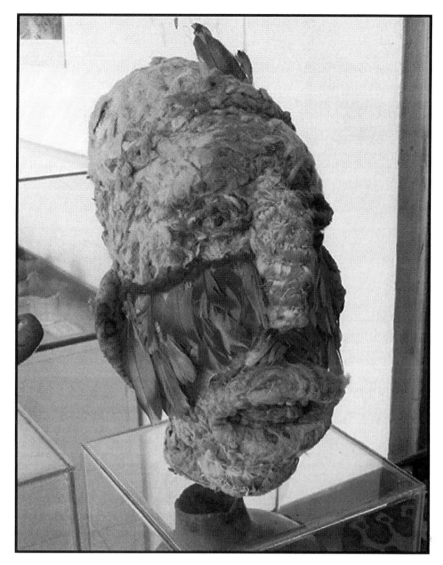

Wool and cotton effigy of an elongated head found in a Paracas area tomb

Another intriguing aspect about the Paracas royalty is that they appeared in general to have had red hair. There are 5 skulls in the Paracas History Museum that have either traces of, or full dark auburn red hair which has not been explained by archaeologists to the author's knowledge.

Red hair is a recessive genetic trait caused by a series of mutations in the melanocortin 1 receptor (MC1R), a gene located on chromosome 16. As a recessive trait it must be inherited from both parents to cause the hair to become red. Consequently there are far more people carrying the mutation for red hair than people actually having red hair.

It has been suggested that red hair could have originated in Paleolithic Europe, especially since Neanderthal also had red hair. The only Neanderthal specimen tested so far (from Croatia) did not carry the same MC1R mutation responsible for red hair in modern humans (the mutation in question is known as Arg307Gly). But since

Neanderthals evolved alongside Homo sapiens for 600,000 years, and had numerous subspecies across all Europe, the Middle East and Central Asia, it cannot be ruled out that one particular subspecies of Neanderthal passed on the MC1R mutation to Homo sapiens. It is however unlikely that this happened in Europe, because red hair is conspicuously absent from, or very low in parts of Europe with the highest percentages of haplogroup I (e.g. Finland, Bosnia, Sardinia) and R1a (Eastern Europe), the only two lineage associated with Mesolithic and Paleolithic Europeans. We must therefore look for the source of red hair, elsewhere. Unsurprisingly, the answer lies with the R1b people, thought to have recolonized Central and Western Europe during the Bronze Age.

The origins of haplogroup R1b are complex, and shrouded in controversy to this day. The author favours the theory of a Middle Eastern origin (a point upon which very few population geneticists disagree) followed by a migration to the North Caucasus and Pontic Steppe, serving as a starting point for a Bronze age invasion of the Balkans, then Central and Western Europe. This theory also happens to be the only one that explains the presence of red hair among the Udmurts, Central Asians and Tarim mummies of China.

Two types of pigment give hair its colour; eumelanin and pheomelanin. Pheomelanin colours hair orange and yellow. All humans have some pheomelanin in their hair. Eumelanin, which has two subtypes of black or brown, determines the darkness of the hair colour. A low concentration of brown eumelanin results in blond hair, whereas a higher concentration of brown eumelanin will colour the hair brown. High amounts of black eumelanin result in black hair. The hair colour of mummies or buried bodies can change. Hair contains a mixture of black-brown-yellow eumelanin and red pheomelanin. Eumelanin is less chemically stable than pheomelanin and breaks down faster when oxidized. It is for this reason possibly that Egyptian mummies have reddish hair. The colour of hair also changes faster under extreme conditions. It changes more slowly under dry oxidizing conditions (such as in burials in sand or in ice) than under wet reducing conditions (such as burials in wood or plaster coffins).

The question then is; why would the Paracas royalty have had red hair?

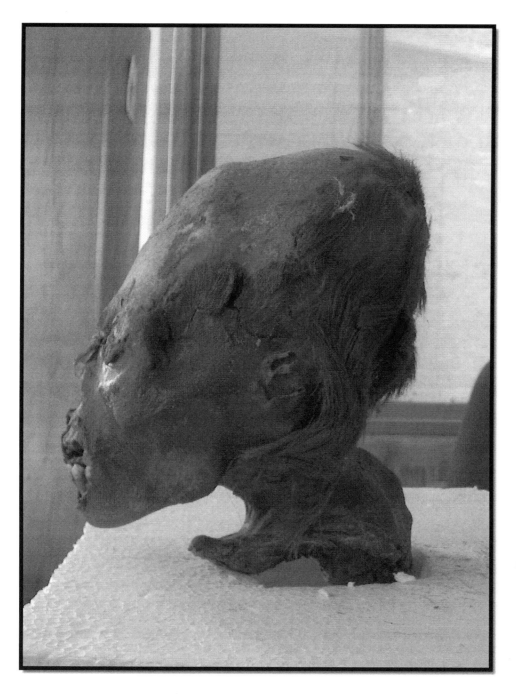

Red haired Paracas female royalty

As the above photo shows, the hair of the royal Paracas is a rich auburn red.

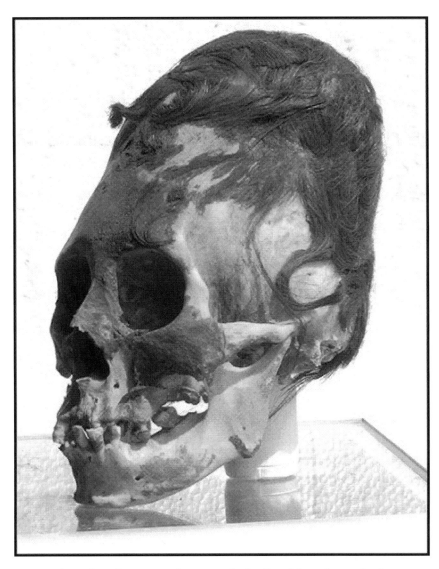

Another Paracas elongated skull with auburn hair

Whether this is the result of dyeing of the hair while the person was alive, oxidation after death, or that this person had genetically red hair is unknown. Forensic testing will be conducted in 2015 in order to determine this. The 5 elongated skulls in the Paracas History Museum which have evidence of the auburn hair all came from the Chongos cemetery. And perhaps the most intriguing is the mummified head of a 20 month old child.

The skull on the right is the 20 month old baby

The age was determined by a forensic dentist from the city of Ica, about a 1 hour drive south of Paracas. Like the other skulls with reddish hair, this one was found at Chongos, and was in fact buried with 2 adult elongated skulls that also had red hair.

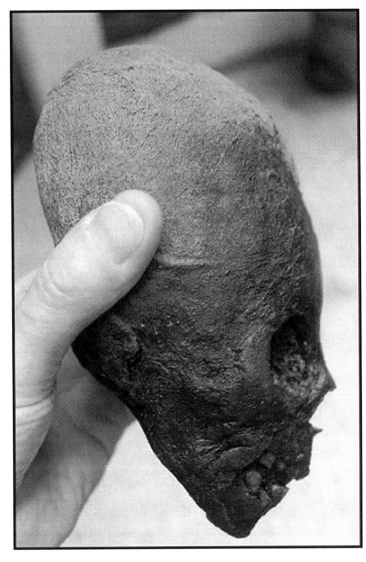

Profile of the 20 month old baby skull

The photo above, which is of an exact cast of the skull shows that rather than having auburn hair, this young child in fact had short strawberry blonde hair. Other such examples of skulls having blonde hair have been found in the past in the area, and thus this example is not unique.

20: Central Highlands

Along the coast, northward, some elongated skulls have been found in graves of small population areas, but mainly slight cases of ACD. We must head back to the "path of Viracocha" northeast of Lima in order to find more interesting examples. In the area of Lawriqucha and Huanuco Pampa some elongated skulls have been found, but of only slight ACD. And northwest of Lawriqucha, at a site called Marcajirca near the city of Huaraz several elongated skulls of different shapes, including "cone heads" have been found, all carbon dated to between 1040 and 1640 AD. (128) The group studying this site believes that 2 different ethnic groups lived in this area, but have not ascertained their relationships with earlier cultures. The presence of *chullpa* towers at this location is interesting, because as we have seen they are also found in other areas, such as Sillustani, where elongated skulls have also been found.

Further to the north, and near the town of Pataz, and right on the "path of Viracocha" two very elongated skulls were found in 2011, one a man and the other a women. They are over 30 centimeters long and are classic "cone head" in shape, similar to those found at Chongos near Paracas. No further information is available as to their cultural identity, or what else was found with them.

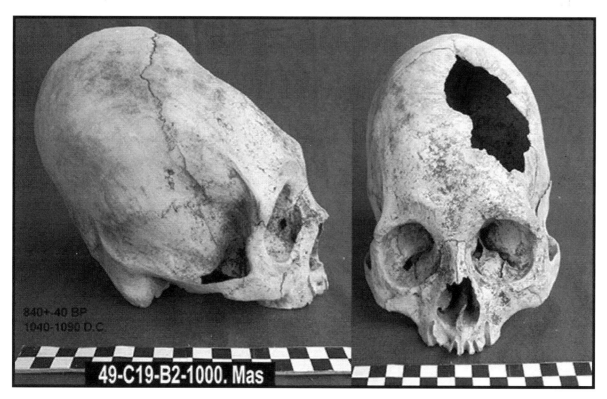

One of the Marcajirca elongated skulls

21: Cajamarca

Our final location is again on the "path of Viracocha" and is the city of Cajamarca, or immediate area. Although there are no photos available, and the only paper found about Cajamarca elongated skulls did not even state their ages or cultures, some interesting results were described. A recent study of coastal and highland populations from central and northern Peru has demonstrated some differences in cranial shape, but not overall size, between populations. Coastal populations are characterised by lower, longer cranial vaults than highland populations and postcranial morphology also show distinction between highland and coastal populations, while there is morphological similarity within these regions even over relatively large areas. This may reflect the combined effects of genetic drift, environmental adaptation (particularly for postcranial morphology) and dietary influences. However, Ericksen (1962) observed a temporal reduction in cranial length in a highland population from Cajamarca which might have been a reflection of increased gene flow with the coast over time. This may be of particular relevance to the populations examined in the current study which were mainly fairly late in date (presumably prior to the Spanish conquest. Archaeological evidence for the degree of interaction between coastal and highland populations is controversial but suggests some cultural interaction (and perhaps potentially gene flow) between the coast and the highlands in north-central Peru at this time, probably through trade networks for ceramics and animals/animal products. (129)

As has been previously stated, the so called Inca road system to at least some extent preceded the Inca, especially the main northwest to southeast routes along the coast and in the highlands. Their origins have not been determined, but we can safely believe these main arteries, and connector roads to date back to the Wari and even Tiwanaku cultures. Elongated skulls seemingly end in the Cajamarca area in Peru, and have been found in a few locations in Ecuador and Colombia, but not necessarily connected with the "path of Viracocha" which ends, according to oral traditions at the Peru/Ecuador border area.

22: Could Some Elongated Skulls Be Natural?

As we have seen in this book, most of the elongated skulls found in Peru and Bolivia appear to have been the result of ACD. However, there are some which appear to be far too complex in shape to be the product of head binding, and most of those are from the ancient cemetery of Chongos in the area of Paracas.

The shape of the 20 month old baby skull seen above could have been created by the process of ACD, as its shape would suggest that; also, it has been radiocarbon dated at 1950 years old, so it lived and died at the end of the Paracas period. But the Huayqui skeleton from Andahuaylillas near Cusco, according to medical experts appears to have been born with its skull naturally elongated. We must now look back into the work of earlier researchers to see other examples of children that could have been born with elongated skulls.

From an excellent article by Igor Gontcharov in 2014 we get quotes from Nott and Gliddon's 1854 book *Types Of Mankind* where they discuss the works of M.E. Rivero and J.J. von Tschudi:

"Finally, the "Peruvian Antiquities" of Rivero and Tschudi corroborate the above scientific view, viz., that the artificial disfigurement of the skull among the Inca-Peruvians and other South American families, owes its origin to the prior existence of an autocthonous race, in whose crania such (to us, seemingly) a deformity was natural: and thus the contradictory materials which induced Dr. Morton at first to deem this peculiarity to be congenital, and afterwards so exclusively artificial, become reconciled; while due regard is preserved to his truthful candor and craniological acumen."

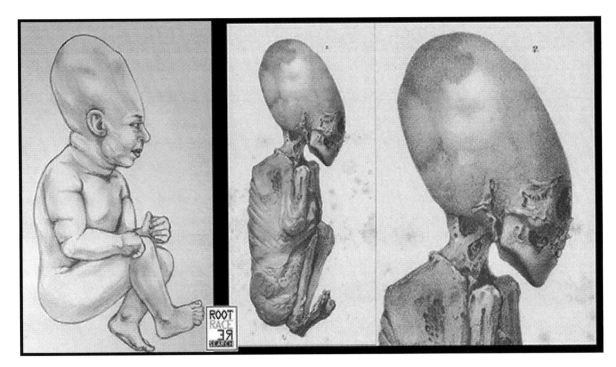

Drawing by artist Mark Laplume

Rivero and Tschudi were convinced that some of the Peruvian native groups had naturally elongated heads, and that the process of ACD probably arose from others, and perhaps mixed blood descendants trying to copy the look of these people. They criticized the protagonists of the hypothesis that artificial cranial deformation was the only way to explain the existence of elongated skulls, pointing out that such views were based exclusively on the observation of adult skulls. (130) They go on to say:

"But, in our opinion, those physiologists (who say that all elongated skulls were the result of ACD) are undoubtedly in error, who suppose that the different phrenological aspects offered by the Peruvian race were exclusively artificial. This hypothesis rests on insufficient grounds; its authors could have made their observations solely on the crania of adult individuals, as it is only a few years since two mummies of children were carried to England, which, according to the very exact description of Dr. Bellamy, belonged to the tribe of Aymaraes. The two crania (both of children scarce a year old) had, in all respects, the same form as those of adults."

The most amazing revelation is in this last quote:

"We ourselves have observed the same fact in many mummies of children of tender age, who, although they had cloths about them, were yet without any vestige or appearance of pressure of the cranium. More still: the same formation of the head presents itself in children yet unborn; and of this truth we have had convincing proof in the sight of a foetus, enclosed in the womb of a mummy of a pregnant woman, which we found in a cave of Huichay, two leagues from Tarma, and which is, at this moment, in our collection. Professor D'Outrepont, of great Celebrity in the department of obstetrics, has assured us that the fetus is one of seven months' age. It belongs, according to a very clearly defined formation of the cranium, to the tribe of the Huancas. We present the reader with a drawing of this conclusive and interesting proof in opposition to the advocates of mechanical action as the sole and exclusive cause of the phrenological form of the Peruvian race."

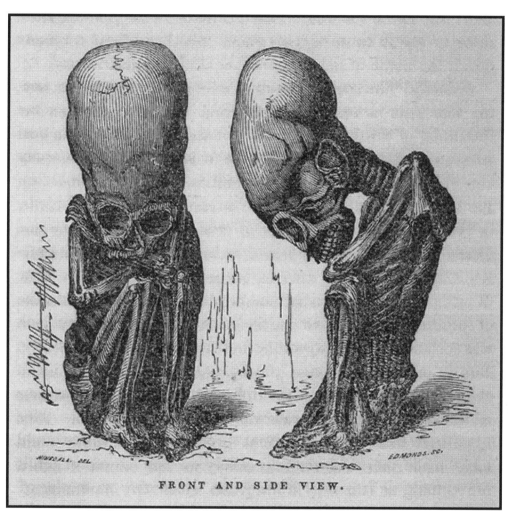

FRONT AND SIDE VIEW.

The 7 month old fetus

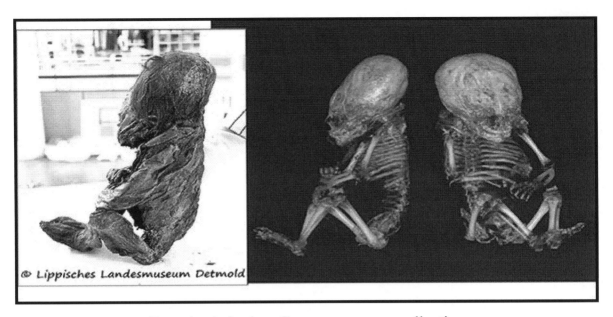

Peruvian baby in a German museum collection

23: Bibliography

1: Anton S, Weinstein K (1999) Artificial cranial deformation and fossil Australians revisited. J Hum Evol 36:195–209

2: Trinkaus E: Artificial cranial deformation in the Shanidar 1 And Shanidar 5 Neandertals. Curr Anthropol 23:198–199, 1982

3: Imbelloni J (1938) In: Dembo A, Imbelloni J (eds) Deformaciones intencionales del cuerpo humano de caracter etnico, vol III. Editorial Nova, Buenos Aires

4: Retzius G (1895) Om kranier af. s. k. long-head-indianer. Ymer XV: 259–271

5: Carrara N (2004) I crani degli "alieni": uno studio antropologico. Museo de Antropología, Universitá di Padova Website.http://www.unipd.it/progettobo/curiosita_aprile2004/antropologia.pdf

6: Lucena Samoral M (1965) Historia extensa de Colombia, vol. III, T I. Nuevo Reino de Granada. Lerner, Bogotá

7: Paredes Borja V (1966) Historia de la medicina en Ecuador, vol I. Casa de la Cultura Ecuatoriana, Quito

8: Moll Aristides A (1944) Aesculapius in Latin America. Philadelphia

9: El Inca De la Vega G (1609) Royal commentaries of the Incas, and general history of Peru. University of Texas Press, Austin

10: Boas F (1890) Second General Report on the Indians of British Columbia. British Association for the Advancement Of Science, London, pp 562–715

11: Imbelloni J (1938) In: Dembo A, Imbelloni J (Eds) Deformaciones intencionales del cuerpo humano de caracter etnico, vol III. Editorial Nova, Buenos Aires

12: Munizaga JR (1987) Deformación craneana intencional en América. In Revista Chilena de Antropología, vol 6. University of Chile, Santiago, pp 113–147

13: Carod Artal FJ, Vázquez Cabrera CB (2004) Neurological paleopathology in the pre-Columbine cultures of the coast and the Andean plateau. I. Artificial cranial deformation. Rev Neurol 38:791

14: Torres-Rouff C (2004) Human skeletal remains from the Island of the Sun, Lake Titicaca, Bolivia. Am J Phys Anthropol Suppl 38:196

15: Reyes Suárez M, Padilla Cerón N (1987) Un acercamiento a la práctica de la deformación craneal y sus posibles implicaciones culturales. Arqueología, Revista de Estudiantes de Antropología UN, No 4, Bogotá

16: Garret J (1988) Status, the warriors class, and artificial cranial deformation. In: Blakely R (Ed) The king site: continuity and contact in sixteenth century Georgia. University of Georgia

17: Delisle F (1880) Contribution á l'etude des deformations artificielles du crane. These pour le doctorat en médicine, Paris

18: Fernández de Piedrahita L (1881) Historia general de la conquista del nuevo reino de Granada. Bogotá

19: Retzius G (1895) Om kranier AF. s. k. long-head-indianer. Ymer XV: 259–271

20: Tommaseo M, Drusini AG (1984) Physical anthropology of two tribal groups of Amazonic Peru (with reference to artificial cranial deformation). Z Morphol Anthropol 74:315–333

21: Friede J: Descubrimiento Y Conquista del Nuevo Reino de Granada. Bogota: Ediciones Lerner, 1965, Vol 2

22: http://es.wikipedia.org/wiki/Hombre_de_Lauricocha

23: http://en.wikipedia.org/wiki/Surface_exposure_dating

24: Dunai, Tibor J. (2010) *Cosmogenic Nuclides: Principles, Concepts and Applications in the Earth Surface Sciences.* Cambridge, MA: Cambridge University Press.

25: Dunai, Tibor J. (2010) *Cosmogenic Nuclides: Principles, Concepts and Applications in the Earth Surface Sciences.* Cambridge, MA: Cambridge University Press.

26: http://en.wikipedia.org/wiki/Aymara_people

27: http://en.wikipedia.org/wiki/Aymara_language

28: Adelaar, Willem. *The Languages of the Andes.* With the collaboration of P.C. Muysken. Cambridge language survey. Cambridge University Press, 2007, ISBN 978-0-521-36831-5

29: Dover, Robert V. H.; Katharine E. Seibold, John Holmes McDowell (1992). Andean cosmologies through time: persistence and emergence. Caribbean and Latin American studies. Indiana University Press. p. 274. ISBN 0-253-31815-7.

30: Alan Kolata's Valley of the Spirits: a Journey into the Lost Realm of the Aymara (1996), pages 65-72

31: "Viracocha". *Bloomsbury Dictionary of Myth*. Bloomsbury Publishing Ltd., London. 1996.

32: Viracocha and the Coming of the Incas from "History of the Incas" by Pedro Sarmiento De Gamboa, translated by Clements Markham, Cambridge: The Hakluyt Society 1907, pp. 28-58.

33: http://www.yurileveratto.com/en/articolo.php?Id=208

34: http://books.google.com.pe/books?id=Gnu1AAAAIAAJ&q=inauthor:%22Mar%C3%ADa+Scholten+de+D%27Ebneth%22&dq=inauthor:%22Mar%C3%ADa+Scholten+de+D%27Ebneth%22&hl=en&sa=X&ei=hRwJU8S2GuTjsASljoLgDw&ved=0CC8Q6AEwAQ

35: http://www.grahamhancock.com/phorum/read.php?f=8&i=18230&t=18230

36: D'Altroy, Terrence N. (2002). *The Incas*. Blackwell Publishers Inc. p. 242. ISBN 0-631-17677-2.

37: *Incas: lords of gold and glory*. New York: Time-Life Books. 1992. pp. 94–97. ISBN 0-8094-9870-7.

38: D'Altroy, Terrence N. (2002). *The Incas*. Blackwell Publishers Inc. p. 242. ISBN 0-631-17677-2.

39: D'Altroy, Terence N. (1992). *Provincial Power in the Inka Empire*. Smithsonian Institution. p. 97. ISBN 1-56098-115-6.

40: Cameron, Ian (1990). *Kingdom of the Sun God: a history of the Andes and their people*. New York: Facts on File. p. 65.

41: Archeologists in Peru unearth ancient Wari city". Reuters. 16 December 2008.

42: Susan E. Bergh (2012). *Wari: Lords of the Ancient Andes*. Thames & Hudson.

43: Wright, Kenneth R.; McEwan, Gordon Francis; Wright, Ruth M. (2006). *Tipon: Water Engineering Masterpiece of the Inca Empire*. ASCE. p. 27.

44: http://www.folklore.ee/folklore/vol12/inca.htm

45: http://www.unm.edu/~gbawden/324-TEmp/324-TEmp.htm

46: http://www.scielo.cl/scielo.php?script=sci_arttext&pid=S0717-73562006000100004&lng=en&nrm=iso&tlng=es

47: http://archaeology.about.com/od/cterms/g/chinchorro.htm

48: http://archaeology.about.com/od/cterms/g/chinchorro.htm

49: http://whc.unesco.org/en/list/420

50: http://openscholarship.wustl.edu/cgi/viewcontent.cgi?article=1528&context=etd

51: Fagan, Brian M. *The Seventy Great Mysteries of the Ancient World: Unlocking the Secrets of Past Civilizations*. New York: Thames & Hudson, 2001.

52: Kolata, Alan L. (December 11, 1993). *The Tiwanaku: Portrait of an Andean Civilization*. Wiley-Blackwell. ISBN 978-1-55786-183-2.

53: McAndrews, Timothy L. et al. 'Regional Settlement Patterns in the Tiwanaku Valley of Bolivia'. *Journal of Field Archaeology* 24 (1997): 67-83.

54: http://www.sharingbolivia.com/2009/04/bennett-monolith.html

55: Kolata, Alan L. *Valley of the Spirits: A Journey into the Lost Realm of the Aymara,* Hoboken, New Jersey: John Wiley and Sons, 1996.

56: Kolata, Alan L. (December 11, 1993). *The Tiwanaku: Portrait of an Andean Civilization*. Wiley-Blackwell. ISBN 978-1-55786-183-2.

57: http://www.travelthruhistory.com/html/historic67.html

58: file:///C:/Users/kalai2012/Downloads/Blom%202005%20JAA.pdf

59: http://www.michaelsheiser.com/PaleoBabble/Artificial%20cranial%20deformation%20Tiwanaku.pdf

60: Ponce Sanginés, C. and G. M. Terrazas, 1970, *Acerca De La Procedencia Del Material Lítico De Los Monumentos De Tiwanaku*. Publication no. 21. *Academia Nacional de Ciencias de Bolivia*.

61: Harmon, P., 2002, "Experimental Archaeology, Interactive Dig, *Archaeology Magazine*, "Online Excavations" web page, *Archaeology* magazine

62: http://alternativearchaeology.jigsy.com/Tiwanaku

63: http://alternativearchaeology.jigsy.com/Tiwanaku

64: http://www.atlantisbolivia.org/atlantisboliviapart4.htm

65: Parker, W.B. (1922) *Bolivians of To-Day*, 2nd Ed. The Hispanic Society of America. New York, New York. 332 pp.

66: Posnansky, A. (1945) Tihuanacu, the Cradle of American Man, Vols. I - II (Translated into English by James F. Sheaver), J. J. Augustin, Publ., New York and Minister of Education, La Paz, Bolivia.

67: http://www.atlantisquest.com/prehistcity.html

68: http://latinamericanhistory.about.com/od/ancientlatinamerica/p/Viracocha-And-The-Legendary-Origins-Of-The-Inca.htm

69: http://latinamericanhistory.about.com/od/ancientlatinamerica/p/Viracocha-And-The-Legendary-Origins-Of-The-Inca.htm

70: https://www.academia.edu/4678316/Human_Skeletal_Remains_From_Bandeliers_1895_Expedition_to_the_Island_of_The_Sun

71: https://www.academia.edu/4678316/Human_Skeletal_Remains_From_Bandeliers_1895_Expedition_to_the_Island_of_The_Sun

72: Stanish, Charles. *Ancient Titicaca*. University of Columbia Press. ISBN 0-520-23245-3.

73: http://www.jstor.org/stable/124985

74: http://www.panorama-peru.com/index.php?controllers=content&action=info&PId=18

75: http://www.handcarryonly.com/condors-and-grave-robbers-in-the-colca-canyon-in-peru/

76: http://www.ninds.nih.gov/disorders/hydrocephalus/detail_hydrocephalus.htm

77: http://humanorigins.si.edu/evidence/human-fossils/species/homo-floresiensis

78: http://www.ehow.com/how_7313415_number-human-ribs.html

79: http://www.animated-teeth.com/baby-teeth/a-deciduous-baby-teeth.htm

80: http://khipukamayuq.fas.harvard.edu/WhatIsAKhipu.html

81: http://www.astronomy.pomona.edu/archeo/andes/inca.orig.html

82: http://www.livescience.com/41346-the-incas-history-of-andean-empire.html

83: http://link.springer.com/chapter/10.1007%2F978-1-4615-0639-3_10

84: http://www.bioanth.org/Dingwall/Dingwell.1931.Chapter.X.pdf

85: http://science.nationalgeographic.com/science/archaeology/machu-picchu-mystery/

86: http://atlanteangardens.blogspot.com/2014/05/ancient-giants-of-new-world.html

87: Protzen, Jean-Pierre. *Inca architecture and construction at Ollantaytambo*. New York: Oxford University Press, 1993. ISBN 0-19-507069-0

88: http://www.minube.com/rincon/museo-arqueologico-y-antropologico-de-abancay-illanya--instituto-nacional-de-cultura-region-apurimac-a437261

89: http://www.limaeasy.com/lima-info/lima-history-and-cultures/the-wari-culture-700ad-1100ad

90: http://www.peru.travel/what-to-do/ancient-peru/wari-archaeological-complex.aspx

91: Liddell, Henry George; Scott, Robert; *A Greek–English Lexicon* at the Perseus Project.

92: Brothwell, Don R. (1963). *Digging up Bones; the Excavation, Treatment and Study of Human Skeletal Remains*. London: British Museum (Natural History). p. 126.

93: http://www.neurosurgery.org/cybermuseum/pre20th/treph/trephination.html

94: https://www.academia.edu/278283/Artificial_Cranial_Modification_in_the_Ancient_World

95: http://www.arqueologiadelperu.com.ar/tcolo2.htm

96: http://www.britishmuseum.org/explore/highlights/highlight_objects/aoa/p/paracas_textile.aspx

97: https://journals.uair.arizona.edu/index.php/radiocarbon/article/view/2953

98: Richard L. Burger, Abstract of "The Life and Writings of Julio C. Tello", University of Iowa Press

99: Burger, Richard L. (2009). *The life and writings of Julio C. Tello: America's first indigenous archaeologist, pp. 1, 28 and 38-39, 72.* University of Iowa Press.

100: http://howtoperu.com/2011/07/20/caballitos-de-totora-traditional-fishing-in-peru/

101: Personal correspondence via fax on February 2, 1995, to Editor Betty Blair, Azerbaijan International magazine for article "Kon-Tiki Man", Azerbaijan International, Vol. 3:1 (Spring 1995), pp. 62-63

102: http://www.penn.museum/documents/publications/expedition/pdfs/47-2/reed%20boats.pdf

103: http://enperublog.com/2007/06/28/the-huaca-centinela-and-the-chincha-culture/

104: https://en.ird.fr/the-research/the-research-projects/impact-of-climate-change-on-the-humboldt-current-ecosystem

105: http://collections.infocollections.org/ukedu/en/d/Jgq971e/2.4.html

106: http://basementgeographer.com/geoglyphs-of-the-andes/

107: https://www.khanacademy.org/partner-content/british-museum/the-americas-bm/south-america/a/nasca-and-paracas-cultures

108: http://www.nwcreation.net/nephilim.html

109: http://aliens.wikia.com/wiki/Anunnaki

110: http://www.sickkids.ca/Craniofacial/What-we-do/Craniofacial-Conditions/Craniosynostosis/Sagittal-Synostosis/index.html

111: http://www.scielo.cl/pdf/ijmorphol/v27n2/art26.pdf

112: http://medicaldictionary.thefreedictionary.com/parietal+foramen

113: http://www.wisegeek.com/what-is-the-sagittal-sinus.htm#didyouknowout

114: http://www.ai-journal.com/article/view/ai.1605/353

115: http://www.arqueologia-paracas.net/about-english/

116: file:///C:/Users/Brien/Downloads/Van_Gijseghem_2006-libre.pdf

117: http://people.umass.edu/proulx/online_pubs/Nasca_Overview_Zurich.pdf

118: http://archaeology.about.com/od/nterms/qt/nazca.htm

119: http://en.wikipedia.org/wiki/Paracas_culture

120: http://www.bom.gov.au/climate/enso/history/ln-2010-12/ENSO-what.shtml

121: http://www.nature.com/news/2009/091102/full/news.2009.1046.html

122: http://jssaa.rwx.jp/web001_kusuta%28english%29.pdf

123: http://jssaa.rwx.jp/web001_kusuta%28english%29.pdf

124: http://jssaa.rwx.jp/web001_kusuta%28english%29.pdf

125: http://terraeantiqvae.blogia.com/2004/122601-cahuachi-la-ciudad-de-barro-mas-grande-del-mundo.php

126: http://www.sciencedaily.com/releases/2009/01/090105120310.htm

127: http://www.huffingtonpost.com/2014/08/05/nazca-lines-peru_n_5648996.html

128: http://arqueologiadeancashbioarchaeology.blogspot.com/2013/12/cranial-modification-in-marcajirca.html

129: https://www.academia.edu/470417/A_metric_study_of_three_types_of_cranial_deformation_from_North-Central_Peru

130: http://ancientscienceartifacts.org/?p=290

About the Author

Brien Foerster has been keenly interested in indigenous cultures since childhood. At the age of 11, and growing up on the west coast of Canada he began carving totem poles and other Native objects. This later became his profession after graduating from the University of Victoria BC with an honours degree in biological sciences. After this he moved to Hawaii and became involved in the construction of a 62 ft long Native sailing canoe, as well as creating wooden outrigger racing paddles.

Peru became the focus of his interest in 2005, and has been living there full time since 2010. He divides his time between the Inca capital city of Cusco and the ancient seaside town of Paracas, writing books (15 so far) and conducting tours of ancient places in Peru, Bolivia, Egypt and other mysterious lands.

Made in United States
Orlando, FL
02 January 2023

28085918R00096